Of gout and yellow hydrocephaly,
Dim palsies, pyorrhea and measweet
Myopia, blues from the summer sky,
Agues both white & red, pied common cold
Cirrhosis, and that wan faint flower of love
The shepherds call dyspepsia - - -
    Ivor Brown gives a gathering of witches

What time the rag Psoriasis uprose,
Beckoned her pocky train & call'd the roll
Mumpish Oedema, Tetter, Shingles, Scab,
Old Belaam Rheum and slavering Catarrh
With recruit of carbuncles nano & ~~enseys~~ blebs
Most loathsome yellow sulpher'd ryalia,
Itch, Abscess, Flux and bloated Imposthume.

GEORGE LYTTELTON'S
COMMONPLACE BOOK

G. W. L. (1939)
in his golfing specs

GEORGE LYTTELTON'S
COMMONPLACE BOOK

EDITED BY JAMES RAMSDEN

With a Foreword by
HUMPHREY LYTTELTON

STONE TROUGH
BOOKS

*For Patsy Grigg
and in memory of
John*

George Lyttelton letters, Charles Fisher memoir, and Foreword
© Humphrey Lyttelton 2002

Rupert Hart-Davis letters
© the estate of Sir Rupert Hart-Davis 2002

ISBN 0 9529534 8 X

Published by Stone Trough Books
The Old Rectory, Settrington, York YO17 8NP

Printed and bound by Smith Settle Ltd, Otley, West Yorkshire

CONTENTS

ILLUSTRATIONS

FOREWORD

For many years of his life, my father kept a large, blue, hard-back notebook in which he wrote, in his elegant but rapid italic handwriting, things which he read or heard that impressed, amused, moved or, sometimes, exasperated him. When he died, the book came into my possession briefly before I passed it to his nephew Charles, Viscount Cobham, at the Lyttelton family home at Hagley in Worcestershire, the destination which we, his family, were sure he intended. For some vague purpose, I had copies typed before letting it go.

Now, that subliminal purpose is revealed and this book is, to us his family, the happy result. We were aware that he kept a Commonplace Book, but it seemed to belong less to us than to the circle of friends and family (Charles Cobham among them) with whom he shared such things in voluminous correspondence. However, once revealed, there was little in the contents that would have surprised us. We have known since childhood that inside the eminent schoolmaster was a perpetual schoolboy, frequently let out, whose very un-commonplace enthusiams often exceeded our own.

So we are not surprised by the seemingly random inclusion here of the vital statistics of the elephant, in the light of a long-remembered visit to the annual Suffolk Show. He insisted that we should go with him expressly to see a Suffolk Punch cart-horse whose cause he had espoused, though he was by no stretch of the imagination a horseman. Naunton Prince had won the championship several years in a row and was expected to win again. To us, one Suffolk Punch looked very much like another as they lumbered past, but he fanned the faint embers of our expectation by assuring us that we would know the champion as soon as we saw him. And, sure enough, when Naunton Prince did heave in sight, we had to acknowledge that, in the spring of his step and the magnificent arch of his neck, he was several cuts above the others.

A year later, when the muscle-bound champion collapsed and died, my father was much affected. He cut out the photograph that appeared in the horse's obituary in the newspaper and framed it, keeping it on his study mantelpiece until the day he died and leaving it for me to keep as a fading memento. Naunton Prince was rivalled in his affections only by Greta Garbo, at the climax of whose tragic movies he would reveal his emotion by standing up, clearing his throat noisily and putting on his rain-coat.

Some schoolboy-ish items in his commonplace jottings would, I think, have been kept from the female members of the family at the time he wrote them down. One morning, when he and I were the only males present at a crowded breakfast-table, he was reading the newspaper when he was suddenly convulsed with laughter. He would not say out loud what item had caused it, but tore off a blank piece of paper and wrote on it, folding it carefully and passing it down the table to me with the strict injunction that no one else was to see it. I opened it and it read 'The Foreign Minister of South Korea is called Mr Bum Suk Lee.'

I look forward to exploring this variegated anthology once again, my enjoyment enhanced by the certainty that he would have loved the idea of it being published—once he was safely out of the way.

HUMPHREY LYTTELTON

INTRODUCTION

'I have marked about twenty things for immortal
embalmment in my book (why is it called a
commonplace book when practically nothing in it
is commonplace ?)'
GWL to Rupert Hart-Davis, 8 May 1958

Two years ago a typescript of George Lyttelton's commonplace
book came to light in the late Sir Rupert Hart-Davis's library.
When he died his books were shipped to the University of
Oklahoma, but this remained behind.

George Lyttelton (1883-1962), a master at Eton for twenty-
six years and a housemaster, was not widely known until the
success of the *Lyttelton Hart-Davis Letters* which came out year
by year between 1978 and 1984. He had co-edited the *Eton
Poetry Book* with C. A. Alington in 1925 but appears to have
been without professional or literary ambition. In 1955, ten years
after his retirement to Suffolk, he began the weekly exchange
of letters with Hart-Davis, a London publisher twenty-four years
his junior.

Both men kept commonplace books and enjoyed copying
things into them.

In his English 'extra studies' class at Eton ('extra' because it
was available to older boys who by then had begun to specialize
in other subjects) Lyttelton had particularly encouraged them
to learn poetry by heart. If they managed to recite two hundred
consecutive lines of English verse, they were excused an Early
School. A roll-call of distinguished men received their literary
initiation in those classes. Hart-Davis remembered that 'his
enthusiasm for teaching and for literature was infectious, his
taste so sure, his jokes so amusing, that all his pupils on this

9

course were stimulated to unusual efforts in an attempt to please him and approach his high standards.'

At Eton football matches each side was allowed to choose its own umpire and GWL was often chosen. If his side won and were given a celebratory supper afterwards, he would have to make an after-dinner speech. The contents of this commonplace book show why in this role he was so memorable and entertaining.

A surprisingly small proportion of the entries also occur in *The Lyttelton Hart-Davis Letters*. That correspondence has sometimes been criticised as two literary buffs showing off to each other, but in view of the breadth and critical acuity of Lyttelton's reading as evidenced here, there is very little showing off—there might have been much more.

The original book has required some pruning, mainly of passages that are too well-known or whose point is now obscure. The entries were alphabetical but have now been re-arranged more or less by theme, also alphabetically for easy reference.

Two Appendices follow the Commonplace Book. The first, GWL's memoir of his friend Charles Fisher (killed in the Battle of Jutland), provides a sample of his own writing. In the second he is in his more familiar role as letter-writer, in exchanges with Rupert Hart-Davis before they began on the main correspondence.

J. E. R.
G. E. R.

THE COMMONPLACE BOOK

THE COMMONPLACE BOOK

～

Advertisements

Lost! One very old and dearly loved Yak's head, complete with horns. Owner wishes recovery for sentimental reasons.

Cambrian News

A tiger skin rug. Head mounted, with fierce snarl. Ideal for nursery.

Advert in 'Recorder' (reported in 'News of the World')

Author writing on reincarnation invites letters from those with experience of same.
Daily Telegraph

Medical man in Cheltenham can accommodate one female resident patient. Epileptic churchwoman preferred.

This particularly pleased Max Beerbohm

Delightful, Bawdy, Wonderful, Amoral, Indecent.

Notice at Strand Theatre, advertising
Wolf Mankowitz's musical 'Belle' in 1961. (Sense of values)

Carols, with no reference to the Nativity.

Teacher's World' (from Belloc's letters)

～

aphorisms

A mixture of a lie doth ever add pleasure.   *Bacon*

The nobler a soul is, the more objects of compassion it hath.
                    Id. (over John Morley's mantelpiece)

Blake called Bacon's essays 'good advice for Satan's kingdom'
and, referring to their worldly practicality, called them 'the
wisdom of rats and foxes.'

Children and subjects are much seldomer in the wrong than
parents and kings.   *Chesterfield*

He that leaves nothing to chance will do few things ill, but he
will do very few things.   *Halifax (the Trimmer)*

Hope is generally a wrong guide, though it is very good company
by the way.   *Id.*

The vanity of teaching often tempteth a man to forget he is a
blockhead.   *Id.*

Tomorrow is an old deceiver, but his cheat never grows stale.
                    Johnson

That observation which is called knowledge of the world will
be found much more frequently to make men cunning than good.
                    Id.

Nothing is more common than mutual dislike where mutual admiration is particularly expected. *Id.*

There are few things that we are so unwilling to give up, even in advanced age, as the supposition that we still have the power of ingratiating ourselves with the fair sex. *Id.*

I cannot believe in the profundity of the secrets which are safely locked in the bosoms of stockbrokers from Surbiton.
Cecil Chesterton on Freemasonry

With stupidity and sound digestion man may front much.
Carlyle

Experience is a good teacher but her fees are very high.
Dean Inge

Remember, the head cannot assimilate more than the seat can endure. *Churchill on after-dinner speaking*

To profit from good advice requires more wisdom than to give it. *J. Churton Collins*

One should always consult experts—and always distrust them.
F. L. Lucas

L'art de savoir mettre en oeuvre de médiocres qualités donne souvent plus de réputation que le véritable mérite.
Abbé de la Roche

aphorisms

Il ne faut rien faire que de raisonnable, mais il faut bien se garder de faire toutes les choses qui le sont.   *Montesquieu*

Rien ne persuade tant les gens qui ont peu de sens que ce qu'ils n'entendent pas.   *Cardinal de Retz*

On a presque souvent un peu des qualités qu'on admire: et presque toujours celles qu'on déteste.   *Abbé de Monfichet*

Il n'y a rien qui s'arrange aussi facilement que les faits.
Talleyrand

~

THE ARTS

Take endless pains and make something that looks effortless.
M. Angelo

Fuseli said that a beggar in the hands of M. Angelo 'rose, the patriarch of poverty.'

Zeuxis was said to have painted grapes on a boy's head so well that the birds came and pecked them. Sir G. Kneller said that if the boy too had been well painted the birds wouldn't have dared approach.

It was touching to see Alma Tadema's delight on finding (in the Grafton Gallery) pictures demonstrably worse than his own.
Edward Marsh

16

Roger Fry lecturing about composition of large religious master-piece . . . indicating with long wooden pointer the presiding figure of God the Father, began 'Now this important mass . . .'
William Plomer : 'At Home'

The French Louvre authorities were using some new device for cleaning, and burnt off all the varnish, though paint and canvas were undamaged. They staged a sham theft, hid the picture until the excitement blew over (and the varnish was dry), and then returned it intact.
Sir Kenneth Clark on what happened to the Mona Lisa

Lady's portrait by Picasso stopped at frontier. 'How can we let pass what is clearly a plan of the fortifications of Madrid?'
Edward Marsh

I am at least quit of Athens with its stupid classic Acropolis and smashed pillars. *Bernard Shaw to Ellen Terry*

Shelley's description of the statues in the Temple of Prometheus:
> Praxitelean shapes whose marble smiles
> Fill the hushed air with everlasting love.

Mayor of Lancashire town, presented with nude statues, protested: 'Art is art and nothing can be done to prevent it, but there is the Mayoress's decency to be considered.'

William Morris said St Peter's was the ugliest building in the world after St Paul's.

They see great cities and wild regions; they are in the marts of commerce, or amid the islands of the South; they gaze at Pompey's pillar or on the Andes; and nothing which meets them carries them, forward or backward, to any idea beyond itself. Nothing has a drift or a relation; nothing has a history or a promise. Everything stands by itself, and comes and goes in its turn, like the shifting scenes of a show, which leaves the spectator where he was.

J. H. Newman, prophetic re. cinema, television, etc.

The true work of art is the one which the seventh wave of genius throws up the beach where the undertow of time cannot drag it back. *Palinurus*

An incident (or fact) has no value in itself, it is exactly as interesting as the artist can make it.

P. Lubbock in (& of!) 'Earlham'

The break-up of the small patterns of living, the levelling of local life and its absorption into larger patterns have turned characters into citizens.

V. S. Pritchett on the dearth of comic writing

A society of *poor* gentlemen upon whose hands time lies heavy is absolutely necessary to art and literature. *J. B. Yeats*

All art is at once surface and symbol. *Oscar Wilde*

Giardini, asked how long he took to learn the fiddle, said 'twelve hours a day for twenty years'. Paganini used to practise a passage for ten hours on end. Monet painted a haystack eighty-three times.

To get Mendelssohn out of bed a friend would play an unresolved chord on the floor below.

Blue Danube waltz earned £15. Irving Berlin's 'Tophat' £80,000. Beethoven's Violin Concerto a failure till Joachim. Toscanini never had a score before him (10,000 performances).

Sullivan told Melba she would never have a big enough voice to be a pro.

The civilised are those who get more out of life than the uncivilised, and for this the uncivilised have not forgiven them.

Palinurus

The goal of all cultures is to decay through over-civilisation; the factors of decadence,—luxury, scepticism, weariness and superstition,—are constant. The civilisation of one epoch becomes the manure of the next.

Id.

All passes, Art alone Enduring stays to us;
The bust outlasts the throne—the coin Tiberius

Austin Dobson

~

Addison composed walking to and fro in a large room, a bottle of wine at each end. Barham had a cat on each shoulder. Dumas *aîné* wrote novels on blue paper, articles on pink, poetry on yellow, and wouldn't use same pen for novel and play. He received Wagner dressed in plumed helmet, life-belt and flowered Japanese dressing-gown—and put on woollen socks for love-scenes. Conrad wrote every book about six times; P. Oppenheim used to dictate three books at once, Handel always composed in court dress, and Emerson wrote his essay on M. Angelo in a coat he had bought in Florence.   *Leonard Alston*

Next Thursday I shall be delivered to the World, for whose inconstant and malicious levity I am coolly but firmly prepared.
Gibbon to his stepmother
just before the publication of 'Decline and Fall'

Sixteen kisses are mentioned in Jane Austen's novels, not one exchanged by a pair of lovers. Sex never intrudes.

Arnold Bennett, after his mother's funeral, said something in the chapel could be made into a fine story. As Balzac had said to a bereaved friend on leaving the graveside, 'Getting back to serious things, who will marry Eugénie Grandet?'
Reginald Pound

He notes on the same occasion, 'Sham brass handles on the coffin: horrible lettering.'   *Id.*

. . . a dreadful voice and manner . . . seems not possessed of any benevolence, and beyond all description awkward, and more beastly in his dress and person than anything I ever beheld. He feeds hastily and ferociously and eats quantities most unthankfully ... As to Boswell, he appears a low-bred kind of being.

Mrs Harris on Johnson

Gray had a notion that he could not write but at certain times, or happy moments; a fantastic foppery, to which my kindness for a man of learning and virtue wishes him to have been superior. *Johnson on Gray*

He told stories with great felicity, and delighted in doing what he knew himself to do well; he was therefore captivated by the respectful silence of a steady listener, and told the same tales too often. *Johnson on Swift*

Coleridge thought it would be 'singularly desirable to try the effect of animal magnetism on a sick Indian.'

Coleridge was shown in an inn a paper which reported his suicide—a man who hanged himself having on a shirt with S. T. Coleridge on it—to which Coleridge said he wasn't surprised as he 'seldom travelled without losing a shirt or two.'

Darwin found a rare beetle and picked it up—then saw a rarer, and hands being full popped it in his mouth.

When Dickens read the account of Sikes's murder of Nancy,

12 – 20 women fainted, and his pulse rose from 72 to 110 or 120. He made by the readings £45,000 in 423 readings.

Ruskin said he often kissed rocks, seldom flowers 'not being sure that they would like it', and once 'gave a reverent little kiss to a young sapling that was behaving beautifully in an awkward chink between two great big ones that were ill-treating it.'

Shaw was charming with one person, fidgety with two, and stood on his head with four.   *Baldwin*

When writing *Far from the Madding Crowd*, if out of doors an idea came to him, Hardy would write on large dead leaves, white chips left by the woodcutters, or pieces of stone or slate that came to hand.   *Lionel Stevenson*

I find Elizabeth B. a little trying. She is so full of what she said to eminent men in far-off places about nothing in particular.
                                    H. J. Laski on Elizabeth Bibesco

It was like watching someone organise her own immortality. Every phrase and gesture was studied. Now and again when she said something a little out of the ordinary she wrote it down herself in a notebook.
                                    H. J. Laski on Virginia Woolf

~

I am so fair that whereso'er I wend
Men yearn with strange desire to kiss my face,
Stretch out their hands to touch me as I pass,
And women follow me from place to place.

The sleepy kine move round me in desire
And press their oozy lips upon my hair,
Toads kiss my feet and creatures of the mire,
The snails will leave their shells to watch me there.

Richard Le Gallienne

She with her body bright sprinkles the waters white
Which flee from her fair form, and flee in vain,
Dyed with the dear unutterable sight,
And circles out her beauties to the circling main.

Sidney Dobell : 'A Girl Bathing'

Before my tale of days is told,
O may I watch on reverent knees,
The Unknown Beauty once unfold
The magic of her mysteries.

Before I die, O may I see,
Clasp'd in her violet girdle, Spring;
May April breezes blow to me
Songs that the youngest poets sing !

Old eyes are dull to sights unseen,
Old ears are deaf to songs unsung,
But if the heart stays warm and green
Perchance the senses may keep young.

Howe'er it be, I will not quail
To tell the lapse of years like sand;
My faith in beauty shall not fail
Because I fail to understand.

New arts, new raptures, new desires
Will stir the newborn souls of men;

New fingers smite new-fashioned lyres,—
And, O ! may I be listening then.

The centaur crashes thro' the wood,
And shoots his arrow there and thus:
Shall I prefer my solitude
Because his form be fabulous?

Shall I reject the green and rose
Of opals, with their shifting flame,
Because the classic diamond glows
With lustre that is still the same?

Change is the pulse of life on earth;
The artist dies, but Art lives on;
New rhapsodies are ripe for birth,
When every rhapsodist seems gone.

So, if I pray for length of days,
It is not in the barren pride
That looks behind itself and says
'The past alone is deified !'

Nay, humbly, shrinkingly, in dread
Of fires too splendid to be borne,—
In expectation lest my head
Be from its Orphic shoulders torn,—

I wait, till, down the eastern sky
Muses, like Maenads in a throng,
Sweep my decayed traditions by
In startling tones of unknown song.

So, to my day's extremity,
May I, in patience infinite,
Attend the beauty that must be,
And though it slay me, welcome it.

Edmund Gosse : 'Epilogue'

Spiritual beauty ... is the radiant power which, defying all laws
of aesthetics, makes the beloved face, for the lover, the most
beautiful in the world, and which, in fact, does invest the faces

of those who are loved with a visible new beauty. It eclipses what without it would be ugliness and it transfigures the bleachings and shrinkings of old age. It is the immaculate child of all true affection. It is the majesty enveloping the humility of prayer. It is the candid illumination of friendship, and the unsuspected reward of all selfless endeavour. It evades description but it can always be recognised at sight.

John Brophy

To fight with form, to wrestle and to rage
Till at the last upon the conquered page
The shadows of created beauty fall.   *Alfred Douglas*

~

CREATURES

When Mrs Gorm (Aunt Eloise)
Was stung to death by savage bees
Her husband (Prebendary Gorm)
Put on his veil, and took the swarm.
He's publishing a book next May
On 'How to Make Bee-keeping pay'.

Harry Graham : 'Opportunity'

It is better that the drones be fed than that the bees be starved.

Fuller

A cheetah is the fastest sprinter in the world—about 70 mph. In two seconds from stationary its speed is 45 mph. A hawk dives at 170 mph, but a botfly can go 400 yards in a second, i.e. 818 mph, the only creature to break the sound barrier.

creatures

The simple bird that thinks two notes a song.
> *W. H. Davies on the cuckoo*

Far off, the world can hear
  A heartbeat ticking.
Limonchik, from your sphere
  As you sit licking
The harness in your cabined emptiness
  Hammocked from Pole to Plough,
Can you know the thoughts that press
  Upon you from below?
At the manger, beneath the Christmas storm,
  The quiet ox and the ass, munching the corn,
Were chosen, they say, to keep our Saviour warm
  The night that he was born,
Now, in the man-made orbit, alone, cold but alive
  Limonchik spins, living a novel death
Alone with the infinite, alone with the final dive
  That ends the end of breath.
Limonchik, will you know
  Something that you can never tell?
In the last moments when you go
  After your fashion
To render up your life, and the echoing bell
  Tolls for you, will God's compassion
Redeem not only you, but us as well?

> *J. R. [unidentified] : 'Lines to a Dog in Space'*
> (the dog the Russians sent up in Nov. 1957)

When fishes flew and forests walked
And figs grew upon thorn
Some moment when the moon was blood
Then surely I was born;
With monstrous head and sickening cry
And ears like errant wings,
The Devil's walking parody
On all four-footed things.

26

The battered outlaw of the earth
Of crooked ancient will
Starve, scourge, deride me; I am dumb,
I keep my secret still.
Fools ! for I also had my hour;
One far fierce hour and sweet,
There was a shout about my ears,
And palms before my feet.

G. K. Chesterton : 'The Donkey'

The record heavy tusk weighed 293 lbs—11 ft 5½ inches long on outside curve. A large African bull elephant may weigh over 7 tons. Hippo or rhino 4 tons. Whale between 120 and 150 tons; a dinosaur 50 tons.

An elephant's molars are a foot long and weigh 8 or 9 lbs. It lives about 60 years, by which time the molars are worn down and it starves.

Its skin is over an inch thick but very sensitive to flies, mosquitos, etc.

Man is plantograde, horse is digitigrade, elephant between the two.

In a zoo an elephant eats about 100 lbs of hay per day, supplemented by bran, oats and roots. Wild bull elephants eat 3 or 4 cwt, *not* hay. They digest only 44% of diet (cow, sheep and horse digest about 50% to 70%) They drink between 30 and 50 gallons of water per day (fills trunk then squirts down mouth). It spends 16 hours of 24 eating.

Elephant sleeps little, standing or lying. Its chief among ailments is anthrax (infectious? A man in U.S.A. making piano keys from tusks got anthrax and died).

A new-born elephant weighs 180—225 lbs; height about 3 ft.

The leader of the herd is usually a female. Bulls have no domestic virtues.

The elephant cannot trot, canter, nor gallop; it shuffles along at 6 mph (15 mph fastest). It can push down a tree 2 ft in diameter. It won't break down a fence, perhaps thinking it to be a trap.

creatures

His pet aversion is the common black rhino, and legend says (truly?) that they hate all the pig tribe. Snake venom is not strong enough to hurt 'em. They certainly don't much like dogs; they hate noise like barking.

Female elephants rarely fight, but when they do they try to bite off one another's tails.

In the East it is thought infra dig to mount an elephant by ladder.

It is not a success as a beast of burden, as it does not carry more than 600 lbs. But it can *haul* 2 tons or so and is very useful in tree felling. It can fell a tree by pushing with with forehead; completing the job with fore-foot.

The secret of training is shameless bribery with sugar, *never* harshness. It is not very intelligent but has a long memory and exceptional docility.

The possession of an elephant with a spotted trunk will bring death to the King.
A dumb elephant will cause a drought.
A deaf elephant will cause loss of wealth.
A hairy elephant and a rufous skin will result in the house being destroyed by fire.   *Legends*

Better the cold blast of winter than the hot breath of a pursuing elephant.   *Chinese proverb*

A fishing story was told to C. Depew. He said, chaffing, 'about the size of a whale, wasn't it?'
'We was baitin' with whales.' (Coldly.)

One gorilla can in tug-of-war pull over seventeen men with one hand.

28

The very Nazis of the animal world—cryptic, rapid, ruinous.

Hensley Henson on moles (1941)

Macaulay seen at the Zoo by two young ladies. 'Is that Mr Macaulay? Never mind the hippopotamus.'

Related by Macaulay

The offspring of one pair of rabbits will in three years be thirteen million. Two rabbits eat as much as one sheep, forty as much as one cow. They cost Australia £220,000,000 a year. In Australia vermin trappers can make £100 a week. Rabbits only lived underground when wolves appeared (date?). Myxamotosis in three years in Australia made grazing for 20,000,000 more sheep.

∾

CRITICISMS

How little pungent, how flat, are the great authors of the past before the time *when men saw themselves seeing.* How odious a virtue the much-praised simplicity . . . I want (i.e. Hamlet, Faust, T. Shandy) the looking-glass at each end of the room instead of the first intention and naiveté of the classics.

Oliver Wendell Holmes

The dislodgement of Milton after three centuries of supremacy has been effected with very little fuss.

F. R. Leavis, circa 1948 (still not true in 1957)

It is hard to conceive that a man of the first rank in learning and wit, when he was dealing out such minute morality in such feeble diction, could imagine either waking or dreaming that he imitated Pindar.

. . . This lax and lawless versification so much concealed the deficiencies of the barren, and flattered the laziness of the idle, that it immediately overspread our books of poetry; all the boys and girls caught the pleasing fashion and they that could do nothing else could write like Pindar.

> *Johnson, of Cowley's Pindaric Odes*
> *(after quoting some lines)*

Sir Richard Blackmore's 'Creation' would, if he had written nothing else, have transmitted him to posterity among the first favourites of the English Muse. *Johnson*

An accurate daguerrotype portrait of a commonplace face, a carefully fenced, highly cultivated garden with neat borders and delicate flowers; but no glance of a bright vivid physiognomy, no open country, no fresh air, no blue hill, no bonny beck. I should hardly like to live with her ladies and gentlemen in their elegant but confined houses.

> *C. Brontë (1848) on 'Pride and Prejudice'*

He draweth out the thread of his verbosity finer than the staple of his argument. *Holofernes in 'Love's Labour's Lost'*
> *applied by Porson to Gibbon*

Gibbon's style is detestable . . . (and) his history has proved an effective bar to all real familiarity with the temper and habits of Imperial Rome. *Coleridge on Gibbon (1833)*

Gibbon could take a long stride with the leg of a dancing-master. He could not take a short one. *Meredith*

I cannot imagine that Dr Johnson's reputation will be very lasting.
Horace Walpole (1800)

Criticism disdains to chase a schoolboy to his commonplaces.
Johnson's contempt for ancient mythology in modern poetry; he refuses to say anything of a stanza of Gray's about Mars's car and Jove's eagle.

Behind Johnson's criticism we feel the weight both of a long literary experience and of a disillusioned but not embittered human wisdom. Dr Leavis's is by contrast that of peremptory and slightly acrid eagerness of assertion.
TLS

To mark a man's faults and failings was, for Johnson, to indicate where he had diverged from his true relation to God; for Strachey it was an agreeable pastime which flattered his sense of superiority both to his subject, and to the illusion-ridden mob.
Hugh Kingsmill

And yet the final impression we retain is not merely one of suffering; something endures, something emerges, something triumphs, and it is something that was with him the whole length of his life, it colours every page of his correspondence, it is what made him loved, and what made him feared—an unfailing current of moral force and moral beauty, flowing along a channel of natural piety, directly from the strength and simplicity of his head and of his heart.
John Sparrow on Johnson's 'Letters' in the TLS

'Fingal' is a brave collection of similes and will serve all the boys at Eton and Westminster for twenty years.

Horace Walpole on Ossian's 'Fingal'. He did not believe it was genuine.

Little inferior to either Homer or Virgil; in some respects superior to both. *John Wesley : Id.*

Landor in 1833 said that Monckton Milnes was the leading English poet alive.

'Agnes Grey' is the most perfect prose narrative in English literature. *George Moore*

The greatest poem in the English language, unsurpassed by anything except Shakespeare—not surpassed by S's sonnets, therefore the greatest poem in the language.

Ruskin on 'Aurora Leigh' (1856)

Browning's life sounds loudest and also clearest for the things that, as a race, we like best—the fascination of faith, the acceptance of life, the respect for its mysteries, the endurance of its changes, the vitality of the will, the validity of character, the beauty of action, the seriousness above all of the great human passions. *Henry James*

Lockhart said 'Jane Eyre' must be by a man or 'a very coarse woman.' (Miss Rigby said a man, because Miss Ingram's dress was said to be of 'sky-blue crêpe'.)

Swim on his pages, take his poetry and fine grisly laughter, his manliness, together with some splendid teaching.

George Meredith on Carlyle

The nearest to being an inspired writer of any man in our time; he does proclaim inviolable law; he speaks from the deep springs of life. But when he descends to our common pavement . . . he is no more sagacious nor useful nor temperate than a flash of lightning in a grocer's shop . . . Read 'The French Revolution' and you listen to a seer; the recent pamphlets and he is a drunken country squire of superordinary ability.

Id.

All his bitterness is love with the point reversed.

E. B. Browning : Id.

That illustrious master of cant and self-deception.

R. W. Livingstone : Id.

One more imaginative, fanatical, dogmatic Scot had failed to understand English compromise or our unprepossessing semi-religious veneration of inertia . . . Carlyle was a Gaelic pagan with biblical rhythms thumping in his head and the German absurdities cavorting inside him.

V. S. Pritchett

The story of two remarkable unhappy people who loved each other rather than the story of an unhappy marriage.

D. MacCarthy on the Carlyles

An old bookseller told H. J. Laski that his father knew Dickens quite well. When Mr Stiggins appeared in Pickwick, the local Nonconformist preacher asked him to discontinue selling the works of 'impious and irreverent scribblers who made gold from blasphemy.'

criticisms

Her countenance was equine . . . and her head had been intended for a much larger woman . . . and her garments concealed her outline, they gave her a waist like a mile-stone.

F. Locker on George Eliot

She looks Propriety personified. Oh so *slow.*

Jane Carlyle : Id.

That disgusting 'Mill on the Floss'. *Ruskin*

Augustine Birrell said he had once heard a man treat George Eliot rudely. 'I sat down in a corner and prayed God to blast him. God did nothing and ever since I have been an agnostic.'

In face, in manner, in talk, in mind, he is weakness, pure and simple. . . . He has the beauties of his defects; but to see him only confirms the impression given by his writing, that he has been scared back by the grim face of reality into the world of unreason and illusion, and that he wanders there without a compass and a guide—or any light save the fitful flashes of his beautiful genius. *Henry James on Ruskin (1869)*

He had the romantic's gift for seeing the inanimate world as if it had just left the hand of the Creator.

Oliver Van Oss on Ruskin

I'm an orang-outang as usual . . . I would give up half my books for a new profile. *Ruskin on himself in a photograph*

Isn't 'Love in the Valley' a lovely thing? With that and a chapter of 'Richard Feverel' to his credit a man might lie down and die content! Blunt too is a WHALE'   *Quiller-Couch*

Have you forgotten him? Granted that his own little lodge garden is not particularly well-stocked or interesting: 'Be Nice to One Another' done in lobelias, and too many photographs of Nuremberg over the fireplace: still for all right-minded chidren he is one of the Openers of the Gate.

G. M. Young on Longfellow (to Maurice Baring)

The listless amble of Trollope's style.   *Edmund Gosse*

'Tess' is ... vile. The presence of 'sexuality' is only equalled by the absence of it, and the abomination of the language by the author's reputation for style.

Henry James to R. L. Stevenson (17 Feb. 1893)

... has, in spite of its faults, a singular beauty and charm.

A later letter to R.L.S.

Leslie Stephen's approval (as a critic) is disapproval minimised.

Thomas Hardy

The Rabelais Club was founded by Sir Walter Besant as a declaration of virility in literature. Henry James was rejected as lacking it.   *Id.*

What is Conrad but the wreck of Stevenson floating about on the slip-slop of Henry James?   *George Moore criticisms*

Unlike most writers whose inspiration is passionately moral, he does not postulate that the universe is on the side of good.

D. MacCarthy on Conrad

It is not a book but a diary of a bigoted parson-bred beachcomber who found his natural place with the Bedouins as a deserter from civilisation.

Bernard Shaw on Doughty's 'Arabia Deserta' (1944)

Kipling strikes me personally as the most complete man of genius (as distinct from fine intelligence) that I have ever known.

Henry James on Kipling (1892)

I thought he perhaps contained the seeds of an English Balzac; but I have given that up in proportion as he has come down steadily from the simple in subject to the more simple—from the Anglo-Indians to the natives, from the natives to the Tommies, from the Tommies to the quadrupeds, from the quadrupeds to the fish, and from the fish to the engines and screws.

Id. (1897)

We cannot forget that in his biblical argot he invented the thieves' slang of imperialism.

Van Wyck Brooks on Kipling

It was a very little dose of inspiration and a pretty little trick of style, long lost, improved by the most heroic industry.

R. L. Stevenson on himself

There's not the faintest hint of inspiration in that man . . . You know the feeling that a great writer gives you. My spirit has been fed and refreshed; it has partaken of something new! One could not possibly feel that about Shaw . . . Whatever he is, he is not an artist. Don't you get, when you read his plays, a sense of extraordinary flatness? . . . You are always laughing *at*, never *with*. Just the same in his prose. . . .

Katherine Mansfield on George Bernard Shaw

There's no getting over it; he's a kind of concierge in the house of literature—sits in a glass case, sees everything, knows everything, examines the letters, cleans the stairs, but has no part, no part in the life that is going on.   *Id.*

Mr Shaw is one of the cyclonic kind of talents that charge through their time as an express train tears through country stations, and if your mind be only a piece of straw or an empty paper-bag or is not pulled in any special direction by something else, it leaves all and follows the express until the express drops it a little further on.

C. E. Montague on G.B.S.

Will anyone ever write a book on the vast amount of nonsense uttered with such brilliance and panache by G.B.S.?

Max Beerbohm on G.B.S.

But here I am presuming an average reader, able to elucidate those tricksy snippets of dry prose in which the poetry of the West Central young is written. Here am I forgetting that intelligibility is as darkly frowned upon by those young as are those stuffy old fads of the Victorian bourgeoisie, beauty, harmony, movement, development and similar rot that had been handed down from the dark ages of Periclean Athens and had

loathsomely imposed itself on generation after craven generation of the cloddish human race, and was seen through and dis-
carded only as a result of the European War of 1914-1918.

Max Beerbohm on Bloomsbury

I was born, I shall die, a peculiar man ... I wrote the first serious
novels in English, I invented adultery, which didn't exist in the
English novel till I began writing.

George Moore on himself

.. that delightful backward George Moore. He simplifies the
steps to copulation as Raphael does the mountain in the
Transfiguration.'   *O. W. Holmes*

Like a codfish crossed by a satyr.   *G. Atherton on Moore*

His smile was like sunshine on putty.

Michael Field on Moore

Poor Lawrence! He never realised, don't you know,—he never
suspected that to be stark staring mad is somewhat of a handi-
cap to a writer.... Although his prose style was slovenly he was
a man of unquestionable genius ... What equipment had he for
Messiahdom? He was in so many ways a foolish man ... Anyone
who took him for a great man he would welcome ... A glowing
gift for nature ... but through his landscapes cantered halluci-
nations.   *Max Beerbohm on D. H. Lawrence*

He had translated the 'Odyssey' and then denounced it as 'pastiche and face-powder.' He confused the 'Odyssey', you know, with his translation of it.

Max Beerbohm on T. E. Lawrence

You have shown us that in literature even a shallow stream should be forded as if it might at any moment prove to be deep; that in prose as in poetry, even a hair can throw a shadow.

Desmond MacCarthy on Max Beerbohm

He energised the garden-suburb with a certain original talent and the vigour of a prolonged adolescence ... Keats with a public school accent.

F. R. Leavis on Rupert Brooke

Rupert Brooke in his letters appears less anxious to communicate his feelings than to insist he possesses them.

Kingsmill

You are not an artist except in so far as you disdainfully make use of art for your reforming ends. You are simply a reformer. Like all great reformers you are inhuman and scornful of anything that doesn't interest you ... You are not really interested in individual humanity. Art, really, you hate ... The same spirit animates you as animated George Macdonald's grandmother who objected to the violin as a profane instrument. And the mischief is that though you will undoubtedly do a vast amount of good in the world, you will get worse and worse, more and more specialised, more and more scornful.

Arnold Bennett to H. G. Wells

His method of constructing a book was often just to take the back out of the cart of his mind, tilt up the shafts and let the contents fall out with an exhilarating rumble.

D. MacCarthy on H.G. W.

There is often found in commentators a spontaneous vein of invective and contempt, more eager and venomous than is vented by the most furious controvertist in politics against those he is hired to defame. *Johnson (thought by GWL to apply to A. E. Housman)*

On Sunday he cries 'Tripe!' On Monday night
He skims the book to see if he was right.

L. E. Jones on reviewers

~

ECCENTRICS

The Rev. G. Harvest of Thames Ditton, a keen fisherman, missed his own wedding to go gudgeon-fishing. The lady broke off the match. He often forgot it was Sunday, and went into church with his gun to find out why so many people were there. He often washed his hands in the chamber-pot and made water in the basin, quite unconsciously. Once, at Lady Onslow's he suddenly said: 'Ladies, I am going to the *bogoi.*' He was reproved for this, so the next day, by way of apology, he said 'Ladies, please notice, I am not going to the *bogoi.*' *G. H. Wilson*

McTaggart, the celebrated philosopher, always wore a string round one of his waistcoat buttons. Gilbert Murray asked him why and he answered 'I keep it handy in case I should meet a kitten.'

Sir Humphry Davy very rarely washed, and used to put on clean linen over his dirty—so that often he had on five shirts and five pairs of stockings. When at last he took them all off he astonished his friends with his rapid transition from corpulence to tenuity.

J. Cordy Jeaffreson

Cruden (Concordance) regarded himself as a corrector of public morals. He always carried about a large sponge in town with which to obliterate the offensive descriptions he observed on walls.   *C. H. Timperley*

At Lyme we met a cheerful man who had turned his trousers hind part fore, because the knees had worn through.

Thomas Hardy

Jack Spencer, a relative of the Duchess of Marlborough, often appeared naked in public, and protested that he was 'in his birthday suit.' He liked to collect odd dinner-guests, viz. all hunch-backed, many of whom indignantly departed; also a number of men who stammered. Each thought his neighbour was mocking him, and there was a fearful row, only ended when he blew the gaff.

~

EDUCATION

Man without learninge and the rememberance of things past, falls into a beastly sottishness and his life is noe better to be accounted of than to be buryed alive.   *Gavin Douglas*

At school you are engaged not so much in acquiring knowledge as in making mental efforts under criticism. A certain amount of knowledge you can indeed with average faculties acquire so as to retain; nor need you regret the hours you spent on much that is forgotten, for the shadow of lost knowledge at least protects you from many illusions. But you go to a great school not so much for knowledge as for arts and habits; for the habit of attention, for the art of expression, for the art of assuming at a moment's notice a new intellectual position, for the art of entering quickly into another person's thoughts, for the habit of submitting to censure and refutation, for the art of indicating assent or dissent in graduated terms, for the habit of regarding minute points of accuracy, for the art of working out what is possible in a given time, for taste, for discrimination, for mental courage and for mental soberness.

William Johnson Cory

Education is a way of life and not the collection of information.

H. J. Laski

A mind which knows what questions to ask and what answers to be satisfied with.

Aristotle's definition of the educated mind

The hall-mark of the educated man is that he doesn't know all the answers. *Socrates*

More conducive to success in life than the desire for much knowledge is the being satisfied with ignorance on irrelevant subjects. *Thomas Hardy*

What the people's schools have failed to teach is that a man has no more right to an opinion for which he cannot account than to a pint of beer for which he cannot pay . . . Whether they believe or disbelieve, the grounds of their faith or scepticism are purely emotional, traditional, or it might be, accidental.

G. M. Young

It doesn't matter what you teach a child as long as the child doesn't like it—and does like you.   *Collin Brooks*

Capital punishment applied to the wrong type of child—the nervous sensitive type—may do irreparable harm.

Doctor's speech, from 'This England'

Blake (Admiral) at Oxford aetat 15–23. Tried for a fellowship at Wadham but 'we may safely ascribe his disappointment to his want of stature, it being the custom of Sir Henry Savil the warden to pay much regard to the outward appearance of those who solicited preferment in that society.'

Boswell's Life of Johnson

A Frenchman, asked if a gentleman must know Greek and Latin, replied: 'No, but he must have forgotten them.'

> Beyond the book his teaching sped,
>   He left on whom he taught the trace
> Of kinship with the deathless dead
> And faith in all the Island Race.

Henry Newbolt : 'Ionicus'
(re. William Johnson Cory)

food and drink

A man seldom thinks with more earnestness of anything than he does of his dinner, and if he cannot get that well dressed he should be suspected of inaccuracy in other things.

Johnson

When Johnson and Boswell visited Armadale (where B. offended Lady Macdonald), they supped with a farmer. The supper consisted of—Minced collops, fricassee of fowl, ham and tongue, haddocks, herrings, frothed milk, bread pudding and syllabubs made with port wine.

Keats was lyrical about claret (18 February 1819) and adds 'I said this same claret is the only palate-passion I have—I forgot game—I must plead guilty to the breast of a partridge, the back of a hare, the backbone of a grouse, the wing and side of a grouse and a woodcock *passim*.'

Cheese should come before the sweet. It is the interpreter of all wines and it will be a happy thought to reserve a bottle of great breed to go with it.   *P. de Cassagnac*

'Have ye no tasted haggis?' 'No, but I once trod in some.'

Bob Lowe said a rock or a lobster are more truly and nearly God's work than an 'Iliad' or an 'Othello'.

Only one man had his breeches set on fire, that would perhaps have broiled him if he had not by the benefit of a provident wit put it out with a bottle of ale.

Sir Henry Wotton to Sir Edmund Bacon
when the Globe Theatre burnt down

44

He was facetious and well-beloved. I think he died of a merry symposiac. *Aubrey : Life of R. Martin*

Sir Thomas Browne approves 'a sober incalescence and regulated aestuation from wine', but deprecates 'any indulgence which leads to dementation or sopition of reason.'

In the bottle, discontent seeks for comfort, cowardice for courage and bashfulness for confidence. *Johnson on Addison*

... with his belly standing a-strote like a taber and his noll totty with drink. *Sir Thomas More on a drunkard*

Dr Fordyce, who drank too much, once visited a patient and finding himself unable to count her pulse, muttered 'Drunk, by God'. Next morning he was anxiously contemplating apology etc. when he got a letter from the lady admitting *her* condition the day before, and begging him to keep it secret—£100 note was enclosed. *S. Rogers*

Vindictive captain's entry in log-book, 'Mate drunk all day'. Mate bided his time and entered 'Captain sober all day'.

Dizzy's pew in Hughendon Church had a fireplace in it and a cupboard in which he kept a bottle of port.

food and drink

Three reasons for declining a drink given by Yank:—

1. That it was the anniversary of his brother's death, who had died of D.T.
2. That he was a teetotaller.
3. That he had liquored up only ten minutes before.

The Esquimaux enjoy bread-dust with train oil. I persuaded Ay-oo Kilt not to put any piece of meat larger than an orange into his mouth ... also I made him wash his hands afterwards— which he did, then ate the cake of yellow soap with delight.

G. F. Lyon, HMS Heda (1824)

Pax in Bello : Freedom from Indigestion

You abuse snuff! Perhaps it is the final cause of the human nose.

Coleridge

~

HISTORY

Hengist was coarser than Horsa
And Horsa was awfully coarse;
Horsa drank whisky,
Told tales that were risqués,
But Hengist was in a divorce.

Horsa grew coarser and coarser,
But Hengist was coarse all his life;
That reprobate Horsa
Drank tea from a saucer,
But Hengist ate peas with his knife.

Desmond Carter : 'New Light on Ancient Heroes'

In medieval England barbers supplied cisterns for waiting customers. Drake had a little orchestra on board ship. London to Penzance or Newcastle took a week. Tiptoft asked executioner to cut his head off in three strokes 'as a courtesy to the Holy Trinity.' Edward III probably the first king who spoke English. It was not official until Henry VII. In St Paul's there flourished St. Uncumber, a bearded virgin who could rid women of unwanted husbands for a peck of oats. Among Henry VII's amusements, '6/8d. to a fellow for eating coals.'

Henry IV's feet and armpits enjoyed an international reputation.
Aldous Huxley

The real vice of the Victorians was that they regarded history as a story that ended well—because it ended with the Victorians.
G. K. Chesterton

The end of *The Dynasts* is optimistic. But when someone praised it, Thomas Hardy shook his head. 'I shouldn't write that now.' 'Not write those lines of hope? Why not?' He only answered 'The Treaty of Versailles.'

History resembles but never repeats itself.   *Dean Inge*

1837	Nelson's Column suggested in *Times* letter signed J.B.
1838 (April)	Committee appointed who asked for designs (£20 − 30, 000).
1839 (February)	Meeting in 'The Thatched House' to discuss the subscription and site. Wellington presided.

1839 (April)	First premium to W. Railton for 'fluted Corinthian column 174 ft high, statue 17 ft high'. *But* 2nd prize to E. Baily R.A. and he ultimately got it.
1840	Contract to Ginsell and Price for £17,860 within *two* years.
Three years later (September 30)	Figure raised to top (weight 18 tons; stone from Duke of Buccleuch's Granton Quarry).

Dimensions (steps between lions removed) : —
Pedestal 37 ft high. Column 105 ft. Tambour 7 ft. Statue 17 ft.
Landseer's four lions placed in 1867.

JUSTICE

Irishman pleaded guilty, but jury said Not guilty. Judge in summing up said: 'Prisoner at the Bar, you have pleaded guilty to a dastardly crime, but a jury of your own countrymen, who know you better than I do, have declared that you are an incorrigible liar. You are discharged.'

The defence was encouraged by the fact that the jury fixed his sentence at 75 years imprisonment instead of death.

Scottsborough case

Inspector of Indian prison shown shivering wretch in death cell by Babu gaoler: 'He is to be hanged tomorrow' (pause). 'He is innocent' (pause). 'That is why he looks so peevish.'

Thomas Hardy was told by his father that when there was a hanging at Dorchester in his boyhood, it was carried out at 1 o'clock, it being the custom to wait till the mail-coach came from London in case of a reprieve.

A Pole was fined £1 for being drunk and disorderly. But he got a guinea as interpreter for another Pole on a similar charge.

from 'This England' in the New Statesman

At King's Lynn a man was granted legal aid when he chose to go for trial on a charge of making a false statement for the purpose of obtaining free legal aid.   *Id.*

A man was found guilty at Salisbury of 'exposing the posterior of his body, thereby disturbing the peace.'   *Id.*

Well done, well done, Gehazi !
Stretch forth thy ready hand.
Thou barely 'scaped from judgement,
Take oath to judge the land.
Unswayed by gift of money
Or privy bribe, more base,
Of knowledge which is profit
In any market-place.

Kipling : 'Gehazi'
on R. C. F. Isaacs, referring to the Marconi case
['It was a sorry show, full of stout lying.' GWL to RH-D]

Of Law there can be no less acknowledged than that her seat is the bosom of God, her voice the harmony of the world; all things in heaven and earth do her homage, the very least as feeling her care, the greatest as not exempted from her power.

Hooker

∾

language

In 1520 Caxton was not sure whether the plural of 'egg' was 'egges' or 'eiren'. *The English language, its late start*

To spoil a hen, sawce a capon, tire an egg, break a deer, lift a swan, rear a goose, unbrace a mallard, unlace a coney, allay a pheasant, wing a partridge, display or wing a quail, unjoynt a bittern, unlatch or untack a curlew, thigh a woodcock.

Carving terms

Barb a lobster, chine a salmon, culpon a trout, side a haddock, splay a bream, splat a pike, string a lamprey, tame a crab, transon an eel, tusk a barbel, frush or frust a chub, gobber a trout, skull a tench, tranch a sturgeon, disfigure a peacock, dismember a heron, mince a plover. *Id.*

A cargozoon of strumpets (Sir Courtly Nice); a skein of wild-fowl; a ribboning of plover; a murder of crows; a rafter of turkeys; an unkindness of ravens; a pitying or dule of doves; a blow of tulips. *Nouns of assembly*

The fence done the grass on the screwman who offered him a brace of gipsy gawns, a red kettle, a white kettle, a Newgate Tackle and a prop.
(A receiver informed on a burglar who offered him two single stone diamond rings, a gold watch, a silver watch, a gold chain and a tie-pin.) *Thieves' slang*

'Custos' (dunce) was applied to Eton boy who couldn't spell or spoke English in school. It is the official title of the Warden of Winchester.

Gray called Burnham beeches 'Those reverend vegetables.'

Bunyan made Christian say that the key of Doubting Castle turned 'damnable hard'. The editors of nearly all the popular editions have expunged the word.

In 1828 Shakespeare is changed by Rev. J. Plumptre from
      Under the greenwood tree / Who loves to lie with me?
    to Who loves to work with me?

'God left a hand on her', of an Irish girl suddenly blind.
                Somerville and Ross : 'Mount Music'

He has the whole countryside punctured with bastards.   *Irish*

Lady Tatton's groom. 'I don't like 'is 'ocks or 'is ass or anythink that is 'is.'

  Though the tough cough and hiccough plough me through,
  O'er life's rough lough my thorough course I'll hew.
                          'Ough [?]

Lincolnshire rustic said of his girl: 'She has good walloping hands and a good pair o' staddles and her bustle's a loomp almighty.'

Yan tan tethera pethera pimp; Tethera lethera hovera bovera dik; Yan-a-dik tan-a-dik tethera-dik pethera dik bumfit; Yan-a-bumfit tan-a-bumfit tethera-a-bumfit pethera-a-bumfit figgit.   *Shepherds counting sheep (Cymric numerals)*

language

> When groping farms are lanterned up
> And stolchy ploughlands hid in grief,
> And glimmering by-roads catch the drop
> That weeps from sprawling twig and leaf.

(*Stolchy. Suffolk for muddy.*)   *Edmund Blunden*

Selladore. An Italian poet admired this beautiful English word—cellar door.

An undergraduate attending a lecture rather above his capacity recorded in his notebook that there was a sisterly and disasterly in human affairs.   *Systole and diastole (G. M. Young)*

Baron of beef : bas rond. Barley sugar : sucre brulé.

Bishop, to (verb) : to file a horse's teeth, also to murder by drowning (cf. to burke). Bishop and Williams murdered (drowned) a boy in 1831. Also 'to let milk burn while cooking.'
Ingoldsby Legends

'The darling buds of May.' Darling was a species of apple-tree.
Donne

'Hectic' from Greek meaning fixed.
Especially applied to a constant fever. Shelley used it wrongly for leaves, autumn tints being transient. It became a noun synonymous with fever, and so feverish, and so excited.

Green Grow the Rushes

One : God.

Two : the Lillywhite boys were Christ and John the Baptist.

Three : the arrivals were the three wise men, *not* 'the rivals' as often sung.

Four : Matthew, Mark, Luke and John.

Five, the symbols at your door, was the five-pointed pentacle on the door at the Passover, *or* symbols on the stone, i.e. crosses on the altar-stone, the five wounds of Christ.

Six proud waters (not walkers), the six good water-pots at Cana.

Seven stars, i.e. star-angels of seven churches of the Apocalypse.

Eight bold rangers were the eight human beings saved in the Ark.

Nine bright singers, *not* shiners, the nine choirs of angels.

Ten Commandments.

Eleven apostles without Judas.

Twelve apostles with Judas.

An ambling horse for ladies was a *haquenée*, and so it descended to the hired and so to Grub Street.

Hackney, from France

Pints and quarts chalked up on slate; or a warning to printers, letters being much alike; or mind your pieds and queues— French dancing-masters in Louis XIV's time, when bowing.

P's and Q's, various explanations

Fags : Parcels in 1914–18 had card inside with 'For *A G*ood Smoke.'

Posh : *P*ort *O*utward *S*tarboard *H*ome on liners to India.

Tip : Box in coffee-house with notice '*T*o *I*nsure *P*romptitude.'

53

Laconic : When Philip threatened that if he entered Laconia the inhabitants should be exterminated, their answer was 'If'.

> How long ago upon the fabulous shores
> Of far Lumbago, all on a summer's day,
> He and the maid Neuralgia, they twain,
> Lay in a flower-crowned mead, and garlands wove
> Of gout and yellow hydrocephaly,
> Dim palsies, pyorrhea and sweet
> Myopia, bluer than the summer sky,
> Agues both white and red, pied common cold,
> Cirrhosis, and that wan faint flower of love
> The shepherds call dyspepsia . . .
>> *The Verbal Beauty of Medical Terms*
>> [*author not found*]

> What time the hag Psoriasis uprose,
> Beckoned her pocky train and called the roll
> Mumpish Oedema, Tetter, Shingles, Scab,
> Old Bedlam Rheum and slavering Catarrh
> With necklet of carbuncles, warts and blebs
> Most loathsome of all Lucifer's regalia,
> Itch, Abscess, Flux and bloated Imposthume.
>> *Ivor Brown's gathering of witches*

It would appear from what evidence is available that the act of oviposition is stimulated by the crepuscular diminution in the intensity of the illumination, and the rise in relative humidity as the diurnal temperature decreases.

i.e. Egg-laying seems to be stimulated by twilight and its dampness.

In the Nuts (unground) other than Groundnuts order, the expression 'nuts' shall refer to such nuts other than groundnuts as would, apart from this Amending Order, fail to qualify as nuts (unground).   *Estates Gazette, 3 February 1951*

There are, or used to be, public washing-places where a notice said 'only casual ablutions are allowed.'

The Kensington Council have announced that 'persistent slumber' in their libraries will be penalised by a fine of £5'
                                    The Times Fourth Leader 1959

Baptism: Dancell Dalphebo Marke Antony Dallery gallery Cesar Williams, son of Dancell dalphebo Marke Antony-dallery Gallery Cesar Williams.
    From the Registry of Baptisms in Pedmore Church in 1676

Hazel : 'Glory be to God! All the calendar of the blessed saints to choose from, and you call the poor little craytur after a bloody nut.'

Bevilacqua, Boileau, Drinkwater, were nicknames for eccentrics who drank water.

I called her a beggar, and she called me a pricklouse which vexed me.   *Pepys*

Cosmo Cantuar was a creature that was half animal and half horse.   *Schoolboy*

language

Phillpotts, Eden : His surname 'against his success with us', Mr Tillotson (Boston publishing syndicate) told Arnold Bennett.

Garrick said of Whitefield that he could make men weep or tremble by his varied utterances of the word 'Mesopotamia'. Sometimes his effects failed and laughter followed. Foote said that he was 'like the cow—after a good pailful of milk he was apt to kick the pail over.'

Walter Scott is a jogtrot name, a round faced name, a snub-nosed, spectacled, pot-bellied name, a placid, beneficent, worthy old bachelor name . . . a grub-street name, a nerveless name, an armchair name, an old oak and Abbotsford name . . . Thackeray is a name for a footman, the syllables clatter like plates, and when we hear it, we say 'We shall want the carriage at half-past two, Thackeray.' And Dickens is a name for a page-boy surely. George Eliot's real name was Marian Evans—a chawbacon, thick-loined name, but withal pleasing, redeemed by its character, like the shire-horse.   *George Moore*

Arnold Bennett and James Agate agreed that 'Voglia la mia colazione' sung is all right, but not 'I want my breakfast.'

A contemptible language; it calls a sword *épée*—not seeing the flash of the sword or hearing it whizz through the air.
                    Prof. Tywell on French

Colley Cibber's play *Love's Last Shift* became in French 'La Dernière Chemise de l'Amour'.

French lady wishing to end a letter with 'God preserve you' and thinking 'preserve' rather pompous, looked up synonyms and settled on 'God pickle you'.

Milton's 'Hail, horrors, hail!' was translated by a Frenchman: 'Comment vous portez-vous, les horreurs, comment vous portez-vous?'

The English always love the underdog : 'Les Anglais aiment toujours le ventre du chien.'

Permettez les petits enfants m'approcher.
Cain was very wroth : Cain fut très irrité.
Behold Behemoth . . . : Voici l'hippopotame.
I am the good shepherd : Moi, je suis le bon pasteur.
Where shall wisdom be found : Où trouve-t-on donc la sagesse?
The war-horse saith among the trumpets Ha, ha : Le cheval de guerre dit parmi les trompettes – 'Allons!'

French Bible

An old gentleman heard two rustics in Somerset and commented on the extraordinary sayings current in the country districts, viz. 'Shake an ass and go.' Sir T. Acland explained that among many French sayings lingering in Somerset 'Chacun à son gout' was one.

Do not pass him by or otherwise disrespect him. When a passenger of the foot heave in sight, tootle the horn, trumpet at him melodiously at first, but if he still obstacles your passage, tootle him with vigour, express by word of mouth the warning 'Hi, Hi! . . . Beware the wandering horse that he shall not take fright as you pass him by. Do not explode the exhaust-box at him. Go soothingly by. Give gig space to the festive dog that shall sport in the roadway. Go soothingly in the grease-mud as there lurks the skid-demon. Avoid the tanglement of the dog with your wheel-spokes. Press the braking of the foot as you roll round the corner to save collapse and tip-up.

Japanese traffic regulations

He has a finger in every tart.

Japanese lawyer on some busybody

The professor tells me I must float on my own bladder.

Japanese student told to stand on his own feet

Three foreigners who prided themselves on their English. One asked A. if he had a family. 'Alas, no', said A. 'You see my wife, she is unbearable.' B. 'No, that is wrong. You should say 'My wife, she is inconceivable.' C. 'No, no, you are both wrong. What is right is to say 'My wife, she is impregnable.'

A man and his wife on first day of honeymoon arrived at a place where result of fierce by-election was announced. Man's telegram to mother-in-law saying 'all well' somehow got confused with one giving result of election and read 'got in after great struggle, old member very sore and swears never to stand again.'

A poetess asked to recite one of her poems began, 'It blows, It snows', and an American gentleman interrupted, 'I beg your pardon, ma'am, but we don't call "It blows its nose" poetry in America, ma'am.'

Trollope met a bewildered Englishman in the Pitti Gallery who whispered: 'The people are so ill-natured. I don't like to ask them. Where is it they keep the Medical Venus?'   *Autobiography*

Knoblock, said a man he knew, maintained modern Greeks understood classical Greek. To prove it he said to a servant 'Christ is risen'. The man went out and came back with shaving-water for the speaker.   *Related by Arnold Bennett*

~

LETTERWRITING

There is indeed no transaction which offers stronger temptations to fallacy and sophistication than epistolary intercourse.

Johnson : Life of Pope

Letterwriting should be egotistical. 'The wine must smack a little of the cask.'   *J. R. Lowell*

It is a breach of good manners for any man to inflict on another the irritating necessity of wasting time and temper over the deciphering of an ill-written scrawl which, more often than not, contains nothing to compensate the expenditure. Calligraphy is proper to a gentleman.   *Hensley Henson*

Thomas Hardy knew an old woman who as a girl was seen to follow a goose about to get a quill to write to her lover.

letterwriting

Sir, your letter is before me and will shortly be behind me. I am, Sir, your obedient servant.

Lord Sandwich, as recorded by Lowell

Lincoln's famous letter to a bereaved mother was written by Hay at Lincoln's order. *Hay told this to Page*

Have the love and fear of God ever before thine eyes, God confirm your faith in Christ. Je vous recommande à Dieu. If you meet with any pretty insects of any kind, keep them in a box. *Sir Thomas Browne to his son (1661)*

Mrs R. has no clothes, has not had any for many years. The clergy have been visiting her.

Extract from genuine letter sent to the Pensions Office

In reply to your letter, I have already cohabited with your officers, so far without any result. *Id.*

You have changed my little boy to a little girl. Will this make any difference? *Id.*

Please send money at once, as I have fallen in errors with my landlord. *Id.*

I have no children, as my husband is a bus-driver and works all day and night. *Id.*

In accordance with your instructions, I have given birth to twins in the enclosed envelope. *Id.*

I have been in bed with the doctor for a week, and he does not seem to be doing me any good. If things don't improve I shall have to get another doctor. *Id.*

Milk is wanted for the baby, and the father is unable to supply it. *Id.*

The teeth on top are all right, but the ones in my bottom are hurting terribly. *Id.*

~

MAN

Man is an intellectual animal and so an everlasting contradiction to himself. His senses centre in himself, his ideas reach to the ends of the universe; so that he is torn in pieces between the two, and so it must always be. *Hazlitt*

Man is the only animal that laughs and weeps; for he is the only animal that is struck by the difference between what things are and what they ought to be. *Id.*

Man should not dispute or assert, but whisper results to his neighbour. *Keats, 19 February 1818*

> But play no tricks upon thy soul, o man
> Let fact be fact, and life the thing it can.

Clough

What age was not dull or full of danger? When were not the majority wicked, silly and pigheaded?   *Id. (ed. GWL)*

Humanity is like a drunken rider falling off his horse alternately to right and to left.   *Erasmus*

The people who become rich (in a community regulated only by the laws of supply and demand but protected from open violence) are generally speaking, industrious, resolute, proud, covetous, prompt, methodical, sensible, unimaginative, sensitive, and ignorant.   *Ruskin*

It is the Fools and Knaves that make the wheels of the world turn. They are the World; those few who have Sense or Honesty sneak up and down single, but never go in herds.

Halifax (the Trimmer)

In a century what was thought natural and wholesome may become anathema—like rum and the lottery—but they are generally argued about as if the present view was an eternal truth.   *O. W. Holmes*

I begin to feel that the mere intellectual will not hold its own in time to come against the straightforward expression of good feeling.   *Thomas Hardy*

A mesure que l'humanité se perfectionne, l'homme se dégrade.

Flaubert

In 1913 there were 577 divorces, in 1947 there were 60,000.

Combinations of wickedness would overwhelm the world by the advantage which licentious principles afford, did not those who have long practised perfidy grow faithless to each other.

Johnson : Life of Waller

Bernard Shaw, on *his* vision of the future, was asked what force he relied on to bring about these great changes. 'Oh, human selfishness, human selfishness. . . Indeed human selfishness alone would work wonders of improvement, were it not for the far more calamitous havoc made by human folly.'

We were not aware that civilisation is a thin and precarious crust erected by the personality and will of a very few, and only maintained by rules and conventions skilfully put across and guilefully preserved. *Keynes on the Peace of 1919*

I don't doubt the progress of the last 2000 years but have no convictions as to its indefinite continuance. I see sufficient reasons for doing my d——est without demanding to understand the strategy or even the tactics of the campaign.

O. W. Holmes

The two most important happenings in my life-time are the revolt of women against their natural and traditional subordination and the repudiation of Christianity 'lock stock and barrel' in Soviet Russia. The one destroys the family and the other banishes God. *Hensley Henson*

'Be fruitful and multiply' was, according to our authorities, promulgated when the population of the world consisted of two persons.   *Dean Inge*

I don't believe in the infinite importance of man. I see no reason to believe that a shudder would go through the sky if the whole ant-heap were kerosened.   *F. R. Leavis*

～

MANNERS

Chinese boy: his mistress complained that he brought linen into the bedroom without knocking. 'That's all right Missy. Every time come, lookee through keyhole. Nothing on, no come in.'

In a manual by Férer (1633). You mustn't knock at a door but scratch it with a little finger-nail. Many courtiers kept this long.

Confucius said that the gentleman is courteous, not pliable; the common man pliable but not courteous.

～

MORTALITY

Bülow in 1877 pointed out to Mr Wyndham in the streets of Cephissia a monstrously fat woman who waddled like a duck and reeked of garlic. It was Byron's 'Maid of Athens.'
                    E. S. P. Haynes

The woman who laid out the body of 'the noble cadaver' said it was as white as the wing of a chicken.   *Marchand on Byron*

The fairest flesh at last is filth on which the worm will feast;
This poor rib-grated dungeon of the holy human ghost,
[...] This Satan-haunted ruin, this little city of sewers.

Tennyson: 'Happy'

Great men are meteors that consume themselves
To light the earth. This is my burnt-out hour.

Napoleon's last words in 'The Dynasts'

Now in the centre of life's arch I stand
And view its curve descending from today.
How brief the road from birth's mysterious strand,
How brief its passage till its close in grey!
Yet by this bridge went all the immortal band
And the world's saviour did not reach half-way.

H. W. Nevinson: 'At Thirty-Five'

The answer to the theory that Lincoln owed his repute to his
murder by Booth was given by an old negro. 'You gets shot you're
dead. When Mr Lincoln gets shot he ain't dead at all.'

In the play 'The Assassins' by Yates

Shall not a man sing as the night comes on?
... He has heard often, at evening's hush,
Upon some towering sunset bough
A belated thrush
Lift up his heart against the menacing night,
Till silence covered all. Oh, now
Before the coming of a greater night

65

How bitterly sweet and dear
All things have grown ! How shall we bear the brunt,
The fury and joy of every sound and sight,
How almost cruelly fierce with all delight;
The clouds of dawn that blunt
The spearhead of the sun; the clouds that stand,
Raging with light, around his burial;
The rain-pocked pool
At the wood's edge; a bat's skittering flight
Over the sunset-coloured land;
Or, heard toward morning, the cock-pheasant's call !
Oh, every sight and sound
Has meaning now ! Now, also, love has laid
Upon us her old chains of tenderness
So that to think of the beloved one,
Love is so great, is to be half afraid—
It is like looking at the sun,
That blinds the eye with truth,
Yet longing remains unstilled,
Age will look into the face of youth
With longing, over a gulf not to be crossed.
Oh ! joy that is almost pain, pain that is joy,
Unimaginable to the younger man or boy—
Nothing is quite fulfilled.
Nothing is lost;
But all is multiplied till the heart almost
Aches with its burden; here and there
Become as one, the present and the past;
The dead, who were content to lie
Far from us, have consented to draw near—
We are thronged with memories.
Move amid two societies,
And learn at last
The dead are the only ones who never die.
Great night, hold back
A little longer yet your mountainous, black
Waters of darkness from this shore,
This island garden, this paradisal spot,

66

The haunt of love and pain,
Which we must leave, whether we would or not,
And where we shall not come again.
More time—oh, but a little more,
Till, stretching to the limits of being, the taut heart break,
Bursting the bonds of breath,
Shattering the wall
Between us and our world, and we awake
Out of the dream of self into the truth of all,
The price for which is death.

John Hall Wheelock : 'Song on Reaching Seventy'

I used to think (being deceived, like most people, by the poet)
that old age came gradually and gently upon a man, like mist
over the Californian mountains; instead of which it attacks one
by jumps like a diseased and malignant monkey, snapping and
biting and wounding with its yellow teeth.

Hilaire Belloc

As Life runs on the road grows strange
With faces new; and near the end
The milestones into headstones change,
'Neath every one a friend.

J. R. Lowell (aetat 68)

An unforgettable picture of him in his old age, sitting by the
Woolsack, spitting on the carpet, and wiping it with his feet.
Aspinall : Life of Brougham

Perhaps that's what old age is, Swinny; a little slower, a little
slower, and at last feeling triumphant at getting across a room.
It's horrible.

H. G. Wells to Swinnerton on seeing a friend's rapid decay

mortality

One can but look upon such years as remain to one as uncertain contingencies while old Time with his scythe has his head turned the other way.   *W. S. Maugham on reaching seventy*

'Old Q' was said to have milk baths and to inhale the breath of dairymaids. His death-bed (aetat 80) was covered with billets-doux.

Apropos there was during his life-time a strong prejudice against drinking milk for fear that it had been retailed from Q's daily lavations.

> Out to eternity now gently go,
> Through no fierce night
> Nor clutching thorns of pain,
> But resting in a chair
> The daylight spent.
>
> Then, ever-undemanding, come again
> With all those early things you helped me know,
> With cowslip sun,
> With tea-toast firelight,
> And bring content
> As you have always done.
>
> Now gently go.
>
> *Frances Cornford : 'For A.S. sleeping when old'*

The Holy Mawle, which they fancy hung behind the church door, which when the father was seventie the sonne might fetch to knock his father in the head, as effete and no more use.
          John Aubrey : Remaines of gentilisme and Judaisme (1687)
          (Short way with the senile)

I am far more inclined to embrace than dispute this comfortable doctrine [i.e. that old age is the happiest time] but I must reluctantly conclude that two causes, the abbreviation of time and the failure of hope, will always tinge with a browner shade the evening of life.   *Gibbon*

The surly advance of decrepitude.   *Winston Churchill*

When I consider what I was in my parents' loins—a substance unworthy of a thought—when I consider what I am now—a volume of diseases bound up together, a dry cinder [. . .] an aged child, a grey-headed infant, and but the ghost of my own youth. When I consider what I shall be at last, by the hand of death, in my grave, (first, but putrefaction, and then not so much as putrefaction, I shall not be able to send forth so much as an ill air, nor any air at all, but shall be all insipid, tasteless, savourless dust [. . .]). When I consider the past, and present, and future state of this body, in this world, I am able to conceive, able to express the worst that can befall it in nature, and the worst that can be inflicted upon it by man, or fortune; but the least degree of glory that God hath prepared for that body in heaven, I am not able to express, not able to conceive.

Donne's Sermons

Take away but the pomps of death, the disguises and solemn bug-bears, the tinsel, and the actings by candle-light, and proper and fantastic ceremonies, the minstrels and the noise-makers, the women and the weepers, the swoonings and the shriekings, the nurses and the physicians, the dark room and the ministers, the kindred and the watchers, and then to die is easy, ready and quitted from its troublesome circumstances. It is the same harmless thing that a poor shepherd suffered yesterday, or a maid-servant to-day; and at the same time in which you die, in that very night, a thousand creatures die with you, some wise men, and many fools; and the wisdom of the first will not quit him, and the folly of the latter does not make him unable to die.

Jeremy Taylor : Holy Dying

But for your terror where would be valour?
What is love for but to stand in your way?
Taker and giver, for all your endeavour
You leave us with more than you touch with decay.

Oliver St. J. Gogarty on death

Prince Consort's last words : 'I have such sweet thoughts.'

Here lies, but seven years old, our little maid,
Once of darkness oh, so sore afraid,
Light of the world, remember that small fear
And when nor moon nor stars do shine, draw near.

Walter de la Mare

Obituary notices are rarely candid. But Rabelais wrote of a contemporary: 'Sa mémoire expira avec que le son des cloches qui carillonèrent à son enterrement.'

Those horrible essays in cant and cunning, the funeral service and the graveside eulogy. *Hensley Henson*

R.A. All the beautiful time is yours for always, for it is life that takes away, changes, spoils so often—not death, which is really the warden not the thief of our treasures.

'In Memoriam' column of 'The Times', quoted by J. Agate

Wilfrid Blunt's idea of Heaven was to be laid to sleep in a garden with running water near for 100,000 years, then to be woke (sic) by a bird singing and to call out to the person one loved best 'Are you there?' 'Yes, are you?', then turn round and go to sleep for another 100,000 years. Alfred Austin's was also to sit in a garden and to receive constant telegrams announcing alternately a British victory by sea and a British victory by land.   *(1897)*

∾

NATIONS

America is living in several stages of history at once. Dick Turpin and Jack Sheppard were popular heroes in England in 1750.

Alston

Whitman emphasising and excusing U.S.A.'s preoccupation with material matters, being a new nation, called Shakespeare's plays 'the very pomp and dazzle of the sunset', and Tennyson's poetry 'feudalism's lush-ripening culmination and last honey of decay.'

Who can defend the American accent, which is not so much an accent as a whiffle, a snuffle, a twang?   *Howells*

There is but one word to use in regard to them—vulgar, vulgar, vulgar. Their ignorance—their stingy, defiant, grudging attitude towards everything European—their perpetual reference of all things to some American standard or precedent which exists only in their own unscrupulous windbags—and then our unhappy poverty of voice, of speech, and of physiognomy— these things glare at you hideously. . . . What I have pointed at as our vices are the elements of the modern man with culture quite left out.   *Henry James*

We were tempted to tell him tall stories ... We told him gravely of myriads of wolves and bears, aggressive and perpetually hungry, man-eaters all ... At this time of year, we said, only a small percentage of northward-bound travellers could expect to get through unscathed . . . Sleep would in any case be impossible owing to the mosquitoes . . . Owing to the high intake of ice-cream in the U.S.A. mosquitoes were known to be particularly partial to the blood of Americans. With the first breath of autumn, we went on, the temperature fell . . . so abruptly that the mercury had been known to fall out of thermometers not stoutly constructed; by mid-winter speech became impossible—words froze on being uttered and fell clattering to the ground. The winter diet was little varied; tallow was the mainstay . . .

His eyes grew big with apprehension and he seemed paler under his weathered skin.　　*William Plomer : 'At Home'*

In the Korean war, of the Americans taken prisoner, 38% of them died; 229 Turks, many wounded were taken prisoner; none died. Mowrer writes that a modern young American seems quite lost without his bottle of pills and water-flushed lavatory. 'Our education has been making our young people soft.'

When sanctions were imposed on Italy, an Italian journalist called on his countrymen to desist 'from such pernicious British habits as tea-drinking, snobbery, golf-playing, Puritanism, clean-shaving, pipe-smoking, bridge-playing, and inexplicable apathy towards women.'

But Lord, to see the absurd nature of the Englishman that cannot forbear laughing and jeering at everything that looks strange.　　*Pepys*

In the midst of these false and beautiful Italians they glow with the light of the great fact that after all they love a bath-tub and hate a lie.　　*Henry James on the English in Italy*

Frenchman called. 'No, Sir, he is not yet down.'
Frenchman called again. 'No, Sir, he is not yet up.'
Frenchman: 'Ven vill he be in zee middle?'

Un Français, un homme intelligent
Deux Français, altercation violente
Trois Français, un mariage

Un Allemand, un cochon
Deux Allemands, la bière
Trois Allemands, la guerre

Un Italien, un homme gai
Deux Italiens, un opéra
Trois Italiens, une defaite

Un Anglais, un imbécile
Deux Anglais, un parlement
Trois Anglais, un empire

Un Américan, un pochard   (drunkard)
Deux Américains, deux pochards
Trois Américains, la prohibition

Un Grec, un premier ministre
Deux Grecs, deux premier ministres
Trois Grecs, un cabinet

Un Argentin, un maquereau   (brothel-keeper)
Deux Argentins, deux maquereaux
Trois Argentins, trois maquereaux.

Après l'Anglais, qui a reçu la blonde et le génie industriel en indemnité de la privation du soleil, le hibou est certainement le moins à plaindre de tous les condamnés aux tenebres.

Alphonse Toussenel (1853)

G. A. Selwyn went to the execution of Damiens. They at first refused him entrance. But he explained the trouble he had taken etc, and the gendarme made way saying 'faites place pour Monsieur. C'est un Anglais, et un amateur.'

73

A peculiar virtue of French is that it enables one to say nothing more formidably than any other language I know.   *H. J. Laski*

If only the French would cease to occupy themselves with politics, they would be the most attractive people in the world.
O. W. Holmes

When I die I'll have Shakespeare placed on my heart with Homer in my right hand and Ariosto in the other: Dante at my head, Tasso at my feet, and Corneille under my arse.
Haydon to Keats (the Romantic view of French dramatists)

Fais que je me contredise souvent : afin d'être simple et vrai.
Prière païenne

Impossible venir Mensonge suit.
Telegram sent by Duc de Guermantes in Proust

Il faut laisser ces mauvais gens dans l'incertitude.
Buffon when refusing to answer and put right his critics

My inmost soul abhors the bloody French.
Blank verse (unintentional) by Anna Seward

Persons drowned : 2; causes of drowning unknown : 2.
Russian statistics of one hundred years ago

No Jews were found in Kat.
Entry under heading 'Morality of inhabitants'

The money allotted to the building of an exchange was not
allotted.   *In answer to question about certain funds*

God likes the truth, but is in no hurry to admit it.
                                        Russian proverb

~

That hot-plate of humanity, on which we first sing, then simmer,
then boil, then dry away to dust.
                        Thomas Hardy on London

Too many of the dead, some I knew well,
Have smelt this unforgotten river smell,
Liquid and old and dank;
And on the tree-dark, lacquered, slowly passing stream
Have seen the boats come softly as in dream
Past the green bank.
So Camus, reverend sire, came footing slow
Three hundred years ago,
And Milton paced the avenue of trees
In miracle of sun and shade as now,
The fresh-attempted glorious cadences
Behind his youthful brow.

Milton and Chaucer, Herbert, Herrick, Gray,
Rupert, and you forgotten others, say—
Are there slow rivers and bridges where you have gone
    away?
What has your spirit found?
What wider lot?
Some days in spring do you come back at will,
And tread with weightless feet the ancient ground?
O say, if not,
Why is this air so sacred and so still?
                    Frances Cornford : 'In the Backs'

75

places

Bacon tells of a Spanish commander who said Satan showed Christ all the kingdoms of the earth except Ireland which he kept for himself.

To find a funeral procession preceding us up the hill to Haworth was a real stroke of what in the theatre is called production. Anything more stagey can hardly be imagined. The pathetic fallacy was working overtime: the sky loured and threatened, the wind wailed and wuthered, gutters wept copiously. A mournful bell was tolling from the church, and before we got to the Black Bull, soft, squashy flakes of snow had begun to fall. As soon as they touched the glossy black roof of the hearse they dissolved and ran down it like the tears of an Ethiopian princess.

William Plomer visits Haworth Rectory

Towery city and branchy between towers;
Cuckoo-echoing, bell-swarmèd, lark-charmèd,
    rook-racked, river-rounded;
The dapple-eared lily below thee . . .
G. M. Hopkins : 'Duns Scotus's Oxford'

That nursery of nonsense and bigotry, Oxford.

Horace Walpole

There is no expression of Christian sympathy that I could value more than that of the ancient University of Oxford, the God-fearing and God-sustaining University of Oxford. I served her, perhaps mistakenly, but to the best of my ability. My most earnest prayers are hers to the uttermost and to the last.

On his deathbed Gladstone received a message of sympathy from the Hebdomadal Council of Oxford University. After long thought, he dictated this reply.

76

Oxford is now clearly the noble city of Europe. I hold that it will be made still more attractive by having barracks.

W. J. Cory

This accursed, stinking, reeky mass of stones and lime and dung.

Carlyle on Edinburgh

No tender-hearted garden crowns,
No bosomed woods adorn
Our blunt, bow-headed, whale-backed Downs,
But gnarled and writhen thorn—

From Kipling's 'Sussex' (1902)

Stinking ditches dignified with the pompous denomination of canals, a fine bridge spoilt by two rows of houses upon it and a large square decorated with the worst architecture I ever yet saw. *Gibbon on Venice*

The sea is oppressively elemental and a great fidget.

William Plomer

∽

POETS

What is it to be a poet? It is to see at a glance the glory of the world, to see the beauty in all its forms and manifestations, to feel ugliness like a pain, to resent the wrongs of others as bitterly as one's own, to know mankind as others know single men, to know Nature as botanists know a flower, to be thought a fool to hear at moments the clear voice of God. *Dunsany*

Poets have never got used to the stars, and it is their business to prevent anyone else ever growing used to them.   *Chesterton*

James Agate wrote to Lord Alfred Douglas, 'Milton's poetry flames in the forehead of the morning sky; Housman's twinkles in the Shropshire gloaming; yours, my dear A, glitters like Cartier's window at lunch-time.' To which D. replied, 'Are you not aware that seventeen of my best sonnets were written in Wormwood Scrubs?'

It is not the business of poetry to save man's soul, but to make it worth saving.   *J. E. Flecker*

He was, as Ruskin said of Reynolds, born to teach all truth by his practice and all error by his doctrine.
     G. M. Young on Hopkins' theories of poetry

> Dusks wraps the village in its dim caress;
> Each chimney's vapour, like a thin grey rod,
> Mounting aloft, through miles of quietness,
> Pillars the skies of God.

     A. E. (George Russell)

Scott's sense of inferiority in the presence of Wellington was not because Wellington was a soldier and Scott a poet, but because Wellington fought to win and Scott wrote to make money.   *Kingsmill*

Let me have a loaf of fine wheaten flour,
A flagon of wine, a thigh of mutton,
And beside me, amid the desolation, a comely youth[1],—
This is happiness no sultan's palace holds.

Omar Khayyám : Rubáiyát

[1] Not 'a book of verses etc' as written by Edward FitzGerald

It is not easy to believe that texts must be regarded as *les petits vins du pays*, wines that lose their flavour after a certain number of years. Whereas Byron has lost, Shakespeare has gained; like the fine wines of Bordeaux, he seems to have gathered flavour and aroma, and today he is a greater poet than he was in Elizabethan days.

Edmund Gosse

I have no doubt that Shakespeare was often hard up for a plot, and would shudder now at the praise bestowed on two thirds of his plays *as plays*.

W. J. Cory

Let your Macbeth be chosen for the nervy, fiery beauty of his power. He must have tense intelligence, a swift leaping lively body, and a voice able to exalt and blast. Let him not play the earlier scenes like a moody traitor, but like Lucifer, star of the morning. Let him not play the later scenes like a hangman who has taken to drink, but like an angel who has fallen.

Masefield

When the doctor and nurse came in in the sleep-walking scene in an Irish theatre, a voice from the gallery was heard: 'Whisht, Lady, my dear tell us now, is it a boy or a girl.'

E. S. P. Haynes

I do not wish, however, to speak with any disrespect of that view of the authorship of Shakespeare's plays which is so firmly held by officers in the Navy and the Army, by one of H.M.'s judges, and the manager of more than one large drapery establishment, and is corroborated by the authority of Mark Twain, Mrs Henry Pott, Prince Bismarck, John Bright, the late Mr Crump, K.C. and several thoughtful baronets.

Logan Pearsall Smith on Shakespeare vs. Bacon

The truth about Shakespeare is that he is a world, and that no standard exists by which to measure the smokey tumult of Vesuvius against the Mediterranean's blue serenity.

James Agate

Oh, Sir, he deserves everything he has acquired, for having seized the very soul of Shakespeare, for having embodied it himself, and for having expanded its glory over the world.

Johnson on Garrick (to the Rev. P. Stockdale)

When Mrs Thrale said only Lichfield had ever produced two such great men : 'I am only the gizzard, Madam, trussed under the turkey's wing.' *Garrick on Johnson*

Poor Alfred, he's got 'em again.' (i.e. piles)
Tennyson's doctor after reading 'Maud'

Tennyson got £6000 for 'Enoch Arden' (950 lines).

. . . his talk, which was all about port wine and tobacco . . . He is very swarthy and scraggy, and strikes one at first as much less handsome than his photos: but gradually you see that it's a face of genius . . . he speaks with a strange rustic accent and seemed altogether like a creature of some primordial English stock a thousand miles away from American manufacture.

Henry James on Tennyson (1877)

Delane, Editor of the *Times*, admired no poetry except Tennyson's, and when a reviewer suggested something on Shelley's he exclaimed 'Excrement, excrement!'

There is some pretty hot necking in Lord Tennyson, only they never quite make it.

American schoolboy's judgement on the 'Idylls'

A desolate-minded man: he cared nowt about folk—nor sheep or dogs; he was na loveable in the face—by noa means.

Wordsworth, according to old Dalesman, as reported by Rawnsley

William is reading 'The Leechgatherer' to our hairdresser.

Dorothy W.

Yeats told Peter Warlock that after being invited to hear his 'Like Isle of Innisfree' (a solitary man's expression of longing for still greater solitude) sung by a thousand Boy Scouts, he set up a rigid censorship to prevent anything like that ever happening again.

'It's not as easy as you think'
The nettled poet sighed.
'It's not as good as I could wish',
The publisher replied.
'It might', the kindly critic wrote,
'Have easily been worse.'
'We will not read it anyhow'
The public said, 'it's verse'.

Vansittart : 'The Singing Caravan'

I strove with none, for none was worth my strife.
Reason I loved and next to reason, doubt.
I warmed both hands before the fire of life,
And put it out.

E. M. Forster parodies W. S. Landor

Where Severn under Bridgnorth
    Its crumbling margin laves,
There Tom would plough the furrows
    And I would dig the graves.
And I would curse the nettles
    And he would kick the stones
And one was sowing barley,
    And one was planting bones.
Above the spires of Bridgnorth
    As early twilight fell,
Then Tom would pummel Nancy
    And I would strangle Nell.
My destiny at Borstall
    Though full of 'buts' and 'ifs',
At least is better value
    Than always planting stiffs.

*James Fergusson had asked a Borstalian what his job had been
and got 'Oi was a grave-digger at Salisbury.' (J.F. suggested it
was at least a rise in life to come to Borstal)*

[. . . and eas'd the putting off
These troublesom disguises which wee wear]
  Yet pretermitted not the strait command,
  Eternal, indispensable, to off-cleanse
  From their white elephantin teeth the stains
  Left by those tastie Pulps that late they chew'd
  At supper. First from a salubrious fount
  Our general Mother, stooping, the pure Lymph
  Insorb'd, which, mingl'd with tart juices prest
  From pungent Herbs, on sprigs of Myrtle smear'd
  (Then were not brushes) scrub'd gumms more impearl'd
  Than when young Telephus with Lydia strove
  In mutual bite of shoulder and ruddy Lip.
  This done (by Adam too no less) the pair
[Strait side by side were laid . . .]

Edward Marsh

'New Statesman' competition, to make good 'the regrettable omission of any reference to tooth-brushing in the description of Adam and Eve retiring for the night in Paradise Lost, Book IV.'

                                       ~

POLITICAL

The natural condition of a healthy society is that governing functions should be discharged in the main by a leisured class. In matters where the narrow interests of that class seem to be concerned, it has its besetting sins and dangers. But for the general business of government it has peculiar capacities; and whatever control a good system may impose, by popular suffrage, by gathering representation from all classes, by tradition, or opinion, or the press, yet, when the leisured class is depressed, that fact indicates that a rot has found its way into the structure of society.   *Gladstone on government (G. M. Young)*

The ancient insanity of governments—the mania of wishing to govern too much.   *Robespierre*

political

The duty of a politician is to educate the people, not to obey
them.   *Bishop Creighton*

Democracy is the artificial equality of unequals.   *Dean Inge*

There is a marked difference between one class and another;
but the class which is in power usually behaves worst being free
from restraint and misled by sycophants ... At present it is clear
that the chief national danger comes from organised labour,
though the average labourer is no worse and no better than the
average squire, banker, or tradesman.   *Id.*

Modern democracy lives in an atmosphere of adulation and
cannot understand how anybody can think it other than perfect.
                                                Hensley Henson

Political liberty in a man is that peace of mind which arises
from his sense of his own safety.   *Montesquieu*

A zeal [for liberty] which sometimes disguises from the world,
and not rarely from the mind which it possesses, an envious
desire of plundering wealth or degrading greatness; and of
which the immediate tendency is innovation and anarchy, an
impetuous eagerness to subvert and confound, with very little
care what shall be established.
                                      Johnson's Life of Akenside

Mr Clement Davies's forthright declaration 'You are either a
Liberal or you are not a Liberal' brought down the house.
Everybody knew what he meant.
                           A. J. Cumming in the 'News Chronicle'

84

When Karl Marx died Mr Gladstone had never heard of him.

Many Conservatives hoped, when rumours began, that Gordon *was* murdered in order that it might ruin Gladstone.

Thomas Hardy

Our manner of colonising has given a quite lopsided importance to the material factors in life. When the ancient Greeks decided to create a colony they deliberately created a complete society modelled on their own; and thus from the first the Greek colonies were as fully equipped morally and intellectually as they were physically. With us how different has been the method! Companies of adventurers 'on the make' . . . have flung themselves on the vacant lands of America and Australasia and improvised a social order which served sufficiently for their needs . . . Who can doubt the mental and spiritual penury of the multitudes who have emigrated from Europe?

Hensley Henson on Australia, etc.

'Imperial' is a word of service not of seizure.   *Charles Morgan*

Victor Hugo called 'amnesty' the greatest word in the English language.

The Tory mind has throughout history been rendered uneasy by the unknown, and has sought to restore equanimity by dismissing the incomprehensible either as ridiculous or wicked.

Harold Nicolson

Old Lady Tennant told Wilfrid Blunt that Gladstone's grand-father was a baker in Peebles. He called himself Gledstanes and was known as 'light bap' because he sold his bread (bap) at false weight.

The personality of Gladstone is very fascinating—his urbanity extreme—his eye that of a man of genius—and his apparent self-surrender to what he is talking of, without a flaw.

Henry James

Like one of those spotted dogs who runs on in front but is always turning round to see if the carriage is following.

T. H. Huxley on Gladstone

Hawarden closed to visitors when Mr Gladstone there. The tourists went off to church and worshipped his seat.

Mary Gladstone

He always hits the nail on the head but it never goes in any further.   *Unknown M.P. on Stanley Baldwin*

He viewed events with the detachment of a choir-boy at a funeral service.   *Vansittart on A. J. Balfour*

Winston has all the virtues a statesman needs except unselfishness. He is so wrapped up in himself that he feeds upon his own vitals.   *Asquith*

He was like a great actor playing a part . . . he left me convinced that a political career is ruinous to one's simplicity. He searched

always to end a sentence with a climax; he looked for antithesis like a dog searching for fleas . . . incurably romantic and arresting.
H. J. Laski on Churchill

Lady Frances Balfour never forgave Asquith for 'admitting a workman to the Cabinet'. (Lloyd George)　*Lady Oxford*

Even his dishonesties are irrelevant.
A. J. Balfour on Lloyd George

A gentleman with all the defects of Winchester heightened by a heavy conscience.　*H. J. Laski on Sir Edward Grey*

When Yates-Thompson, a pro-German, asked John Morley if he didn't think Grey ought to be hanged, Morley said he was against capital punishment.

He is an immortal. He has no heart, no brain, and no guts. How can a man like that die?　*Clemenceau on Pétain*

A dark horse in a loose box.　*Morley on Rosebery*

One of those dynamic, semi-civilised prodigies, like Theodoric and Charlemagne, who may be set for the regeneration of society, but who may be, like others of the same type, raised up for its destruction.　*Hensley Henson on Stalin*

reading

To be well-informed one must read many merely instructive books. To be cultivated (let us say to enjoy deeply) one must read slowly and with a lingering appreciation the comparatively few books that have been written by men who have lived, thought and felt with style.   *Aldous Huxley*

Every book worth reading ought to be read three times through; once to see what it is all about, once to observe how it is done, and once to argue with the author.   *G. M. Young*

Reading should be three parts gloating, dreaming, pondering rumination.   *Q (quoted by Holbrook Jackson)*

Reading is the procession of symbolic reasoning, sustained by the interfacilitation of an intricate hierarchy of substrata factors that have been mobilised as a psychological working system and pressed into service in accordance with the purpose of the reader.
Useful lucid pronouncement
by Dr J. A. Holmes of California

Many who read the old classics (of all languages) often feel inclined to say, like Lord Melbourne seeing (or reading?) 'Volpone': 'I knew it would be dull, but not so damned dull.'

> Last night I dreamt that Shakespeare's ghost
> Sat for a Civil Service post:
> The subject chosen for that year
> Was taken from the play King Lear;
> And Shakespeare did it very badly
> Because he had not read his Bradley.

                    G. M. Trevelyan

~

... its sobriety, its amiability, the fastidiousess that one recognises in its swept and garnished cathedrals, resonant with the silvery intoning of Minor Canons and the soaring bird-notes of apple-cheeked choristers, so incomparably more tasteful (and less potent) than the quick mutterings and nasal yells that you hear among the dim, tawdry altars and undusted confessionals of the cathedrals of Italy and Spain.

Raymond Mortimer on the Anglican Church

... the exquisite atmosphere of an English cathedral—the silvery intoning of collects and litanies, and the dulcet concert of choir and organ purify hymns and prayers of any over-urgent meaning; in so general a manner and so sonorous a prose do we confess our sins that they scarcely seem sinful.

Id.

I hope in time to take pleasure in public worship. *Johnson*

I believe in going to church. It is a moral drill and people must have something. If there is no church in a country village there is nothing. I believe in reformation coming from *within* the church. *Thomas Hardy*

> That with this bright believing band
>   I have no claim to be,
> That faiths by which my comrades stand
>   Seem fantasies to me,
> And mirage-mists their Shining Land,
>   Is a strange destiny.
>   [...]
> Since heart of mine knows not that ease
>   Which they know; since it be
> That He who breathes All's Well to these
>   Breathes no All's-Well to me,

> My lack might move their sympathies
>> And Christian charity !
>
> [...]
>
> Yet I would bear my shortcomings
>> With meet tranquility,
> But for the charge that blessed things
>> I'd liefer not have be.
> O, doth a bird deprived of wings
>> Go earth-bound wilfully !
>
> *　　　*　　　*
>
> Enough. As yet disquiet clings
>> About us. Rest shall we.
>
>> *T. Hardy : 'The Impercipient'*
>> *(at a cathedral service)*

It has been obvious for centuries that the Supreme Mover of Movers, the Prime Force or Forces must be either limited in power, unknowing, or cruel.   *Id.*

Sir, God hath taken away your eldest son by a cannon-shot. It brake his leg. We were necessitated to have it cut off, whereof he died. Sir, you know my own trials this way . . . There is your precious child full of glory, never to know sin or sorrow any more. He was a gallant young man, exceedingly gracious. God give you his comfort.

Cromwell's letter to the father of Captain Valentine Walton

Religion is always decaying in the hands of the multitude; it has to be revived by individuals.   *Bishop Creighton*

Religion is that activity of the human imagination towards self-preservation, by means of which Man seeks to carry his essential vital purposes through against the adverse pressure of the world, by raising himself freely towards the world's ordering and governing powers when the limits of his own strength are reached. *Bender*

I wonder it does not make the Christian uneasy to reflect that if he had been born in e.g. Morocco or Ceylon Christianity would have seemed as absurd to him as Mohammedanism and Buddhism seem to the Christian. *Maugham*

Religions like Christianity and Buddhism are desperate stratagems of failure, the failure to be men . . . what should we think of dogs' monasteries, hermit cats, vegetarian tigers? Those of us who were brought up as Christians and who have lost our faith, have retained the Christian sense of sin without the saving belief in redemption. *Palinurus*

Mme de la Ferté-Imbault possessed the complacent unscrupulousness that characterises persons who are religious but not good. *Raymond Mortimer*

Nothing is more unpleasant than a virtuous person with a mean mind. *Bagehot*

The Supreme Being must be an entirely different person from what I suppose him to be if he would care in the least for the society of your relations.

Charles Dickens, to a man who had told him
his wife and mother were with God

religion

Religious convictions that are even remotely orthodox stand in the way of any rational political system.   *H. J. Laski*

Men in the nineteenth century were sad that they could no longer believe in God. They are more deeply saddened now by the fact that they cannot believe in man.

Wechsler : Age of Suspicion

True penitence condemns to silence. What a man is ready to recall he would be ready to repeat.

F. H. Bradley on Oxford Groupists

The fact that God has managed to survive the inanities of the religions that do him homage is a truly miraculous proof of his existence.   *Ben Hecht*

I am now in the land where Our Lord was born. There are no movies and no football, and if I stay here long I shall have to turn religious too.   *Soldier's letter from Palestine*

> . . . And is it true? And is it true,
> This most tremendous tale of all,
> Seen in a stained-glass window's hue.
> A Baby in an ox's stall?
> The Maker of the stars and sea
> Become a Child on earth for me?
>
> And is it true? For if it is,
> No loving fingers tying strings
> Around those tissued fripperies,
> The sweet and silly Chistmas things,

Bath salts and inexpensive scent
And hideous tie so kindly meant.

No love that in a family dwells,
No carolling in frosty air,
Nor all the steeple-shaking bells
Can with this single Truth compare—
That God was Man in Palestine,
And lives today in Bread and Wine.

John Betjeman : from 'Christmas'

To kindle a light for our darkness
        Within not without us
There passed as the flash of a meteor,
        In far Galilee,
A man whom the God in our conscience
        Received as a master,
A Herald who wrote us a charter
        Of high pedigree.

But we raised him on high to a heaven,
        To sit with Jehovah,
And to cast in his lot with a God who
        Had finished his reign,
And dry as the sand of the Sahara,
        And empty our hearts are
And empty and dry will they be till
        We find him again.

L. E. Jones : 'The Lost Leader'

Yet his finger has pointed the way
And after the night comes the day.

Id.

In the beginning chaos, then the Word,
Then light and life upon the planet stirred;
Now, aeons after, chaos rules again,
The Word forgotten, only words remain.

Id.

religion

D'Abernon, when the French complained of four guns found in Germany and Stresemann asked 'What on earth do four bits of old iron matter?' replied 'Remember the mischief brought by four nails at Jerusalem 2000 years ago.'

The world would use us just as it did the martyrs if we loved God as they did.   *Bishop Wilson*

When you travel to the Celestial City carry no letter of introduction. When you knock, ask to see God—none of the servants.   *Thoreau*

Hanno, Archbishop of Cologne in the 12th century, caused the eyes of several judges to be put out for giving an unjust judgement against a poor woman—except one of them to whom he left one eye that he might see to lead the others home.

In 1856–7 the Enabling Bill abolishing compulsory C. of E. 'ship on University scholars was passed. *Two* bishops voted pro, twenty-two against.

Stupid, fetid animals in cauliflower wigs and clean lawnsleeves.
Carlyle on bishops

A fine ascetical coxcomb and tufthunter.
Lockhart on Cardinal Manning

Thirlwall, it was said, kept a large dog trained to recognise and bite curates.

The odious stranger, disguising every circumstance of time and place, assumed the mask of a martyr, a saint, and a Christian hero; and the infamous George of Cappadocia has been transformed into the renowned St George of England, the patron of arms, of chivalry and of the Garter.

Gibbon (who claims that George was an army victualler who by fraud and graft got wealthy and became Bishop of Alexandria)

St Kenelm, aetat 7, succeeded his father King of Mercia in 819, but his sister Quendryda coveted the Kingdom and bribed Ascobert to kill Kenelm. Ascobert took him hunting, and while he slept, dug his grave. Kenelm woke up and said: 'Grave no good because I shall rest in a place provided by God. And as a sign this stick shall grow.' But Ascobert killed and buried him. The stick grew into a vast ash. As Ascobert buried him, the boy sang hymn 'We praise thee O God'. A shining light hung over the grave, and a white cow took up her abode there; the herd followed and grazed there and gave doubled amount of milk (the grass grew with doubled speed at night).

Quendryda commanded that anyone who sought or even mentioned Kenelm should be instantly beheaded. But a white dove with a scroll appeared to the Pope at mass and gave him a white scroll with gold lettering telling where Kenelm's grave was. Pope sent message to Wilfred Archbishop of Canterbury (805-22) and Kenelm's body was dug up and taken to Winchcombe.

More miracles followed. Quendryda, in order to pervert Kenelm's good to ill, went to St Peter's church and repeated Psalm 108 backwards. But at verse 'Let this be the reward of my adversaries' both her eyes fell onto the page. A century later the Douce MC recorded that the psalter was stained with her blood. When Quendryda died (soon presumably) no church, or churchyard or field would hold her body, which was eventually thrown into a deep ditch. Many miracles occurred through Kenelm, chiefly to help the maimed and the blind, and in the tenth century (probably) the Abbot of Worcester ordered that Kenelm's bones should go to the scene of the murder (Clent).

The chapel there is built over a spring, probably on Saxon foundations. Pilgrims were frequent, and Kenelmstowe was a populous town in the 12th century (vanished at restoration). Gladstone, who sometimes worshipped there, gave the E. window.   *From a history of Worcestershire*

Sir Thomas More was not canonised till 1935. His jests on the scaffold displeased the Catholics.

O Lord Thou knowest that I have nine houses in the city of London and that I have lately purchased an estate in Essex. I beseech Thee to preserve the counties of Essex and Middlesex from fires and earthquakes. And as I have also a mortgage in Hertfordshire, I beg Thee to have an eye of compassion on that county, and for the rest of the counties Thou mayest deal with them as Thou art pleased.

The author said to be W. Ward M.P. who invented a pill compounded of arsenic and antimony.

Let us thank God for his servant Neville Stuart Talbot. For Neville's witness in thought and word and life to the reality of God, to the gospel of our Lord Jesus Christ crucified and risen: for the strength and tenderness of his ministry: for his greatness of heart in leadership, love, and friendship. Let us pray that God may grant him his heart's desire and fulfil all his mind, that God may give him the light of his presence, the peace of his pardon, and the joy of his service in the city of God.

May he rest in peace and may light perpetual shine upon him.

E. K. Talbot

Almighty God who guidest the destinies of all men, we of this household kneel before Thee for the last time together under this roof to ask Thy blessing upon us. Go with us all, we beseech Thee, on our several ways, so that we may live, strengthened always by the knowledge of Thy presence, steadfast warriors in the battle of life, but with Thy peace in our hearts. And may the bond of friendship and brotherly love, and all the happy memories that we share unite us, whether our days be many or few, in a fellowship that shall last to the hour of death, through Jesus Christ Our Lord.

Prayer at last House Prayers at Eton, July 1944. G.W.L.

∾

ROYALTY

Rex Henricus Octavus
Took away more than he gave us.

Old Eton rhyme

Richard Brandon, said to have been the executioner of Charles I, was paid £30 all in half-crowns for it and had an orange and a handkerchief out of the King's pocket which he sold for 10/-. His coffin was nearly lynched at his burial.

Call to mynde, good Kate, how hardly we princes can brooke the crossing of our commandes. How yreful will the hiest power be you may be sure when Murmure shall be made of his pleasing wil. Let Nature therefor not hurt yrself but give place to the giver. And though this lesson be from a seely vikar, yet it is sent from a lovinge souveraine.

Queen Elizabeth to Lady K. Paget (letter at Hagley Hall)

royalty

To review this towering regiment was his daily pleasure; and to perpetuate it was so much his care, that when he met a tall woman, he immediately commanded one of his Titanian retinue to marry her, that they might propogate procerity, and produce heirs to the father's habiliments.

Johnson's Memoirs of the King of Prussia,
Frederick the Great's father

A fly flew in King James's eye and he reproached it, 'Have I not three Kingdoms and thou must needs fly in my eye?'

'The Clergy would have us believe (them) against our own reason, as the woman would have had her husband against his own eyes when he took her with with another man. 'What! will you believe your own eyes before your own sweet wife?'

King James's wit

King William III used to visit Temple when he was disabled by the gout, and being attended by Swift in the garden showed him how to cut asparagus in the Dutch way.

Johnson : 'Life of Swift'

When George III was mad, Parliament passed a law authorising his birching. (Modern treatment violent electric shocks?).

To the King's most excellent Majesty, We, the Chancellor, Masters and Scholars of the University of Cambridge, desire to approach You with our loyal and dutiful congratulations on the completion of the twenty-fifth year of Your Majesty's reign.

The events of that reign, for greatness and moment, are such as have rarely been comprised within twenty-five years of human history. It has witnessed unexampled acceleration in the progress of man's acquaintance with the physical universe, his mastery of the forces of nature, and his skill in their application to the processes of industry and to the arts of life. No less to the contrivance of havoc and destruction has the advance of knowledge imparted new and prodigious efficacy; and it has been the lot of Your Majesty to confront at the head of your people the most formidable assault which has ever been delivered upon the safety and freedom of these realms. By exertion and sacrifice that danger was victoriously repelled; and Your Majesty's subjects, who have looked abroad upon the fall of states, the dissolution of systems, and a continent parcelled out anew, enjoy beneath your sceptre the retrospect of a period, acquainted indeed with anxieties even within the body politic and perplexed by the emergence of new and difficult problems, but harmoniously combining stability with progress and rich in its contribution of benefits to the health and welfare of the community . . .

Called suddenly to the throne in an hour of vehement political contention, Your Majesty gave early evidence of the qualities which have since proved equal to every occasion. Courage and composure, steadfast impartiality, wise judgement, and delicate feeling have ever been present and manifest; and a transparent openness of nature has knit Your Majesty to the affections of all your subjects, who, without respect of rank or condition, are conscious of what we may presume to call a fellow-feeling with their sovereign. That Your Majesty, with your august and beloved Consort at your side, may be granted long life and happy continuance of the blessings vouchsafed to your reign in the years already numbered is the earnest prayer of this University, even as it is the common hope of a people fortunate in their King and grateful for their fortune.

> *A. E. Housman's Address to King George V*
> *on the occasion of his Jublilee, 1935*

Note. All formal addresses to, as well as by, the Monarch have to be vetted by the Home Office or some such authority. This address was sent back to Cambridge unaltered, but with the comment 'This seems to be good English.'

royalty

Lift latch, step in, be welcome, Sir,
Albeit to see you I'm unglad,
And your face is fraught with a deathly shyness
Bleaching what pink it may have had.
Come in, come in, Your Royal Highness.

Beautiful weather? Sir, that's true,
Though the farmers are casting crabbed looks
At tilth's and pasture's dearth of spryness.—
Yes, Sir, I've written several books.—
A little more chicken, Your Royal Highness?

Lift latch, step out, your car is here
To bear you hence from this ancient vale.
We are each of us changed by our brief strange nighness
Though each of us lives to tell the tale.
Farewell, farewell, Your Royal Highness.

Max Beerbohm : 'A Luncheon'

The occasion of the above poem was the historic luncheon-party
in 1923, when the officials of the Duchy of Cornwall—rather
rashly—took the Prince of Wales to see Thomas Hardy and his
wife at Max Gate. About pudding-time, a deathly silence fell on
the table. At last the Prince broke it, with a gallant but desperate,
conversational charge: 'Tell me, Mr Hardy,' he said, 'I was having
an argument with my Mama last night—she said you'd written
a book called—I think—'Tess of the D'Urbervilles,' but I said
I was sure it was somebody else. Which of us was right?'

And T.H., perfectly composed like the true gentleman he was, answered quietly 'The Queen was right, Sir. That *was* the name of one of my earlier novels.'

Walter Peacock, who, as secretary to the Duchy, was present, told me that tale two days later. So I know it to be true.

Alan Lascelles

It was surely for such a purpose as the Coronation Service that God created television.   *Letter in 'Picture Post'*

~

SCIENCE

Distance and time taken for light to reach:—
Moon (240,000 miles) = 1 1/3 seconds.
Sun (93 million miles) = 8 minutes
Pluto (7500 million miles) = 10 light years.
Great Bear = 100 light years.
Milky Way = 80,000 light years.
Nebular Universe = 10,000 million light years.

Pluto takes 248 years to go round the sun.

Earth is 7918 miles in diameter.
Jupiter is 87,000 miles in diameter.
Sun is 864,000 miles in diameter.

Jupiter has twelve moons.

The nearest fixed star is about 25,000 miles away.

The Milky Way has about 300,000 million stars and there are *many million* such assemblages. The distance between them takes about two million light years to traverse. The sun weighs 2000 quadrillion tons, the Milky Way 60,000 million times as much as the sun—but *much* the largest part of the universe is empty.   *A few obviously absurd but apparently true facts*

Science concentrates on nature and ignores man; the humanities concentrate on man and ignore nature . . .The scientist explains everything except himself.   *R. W. Livingstone*

He delighted in the methods of science; but on curiosity alone he could not live. When the results of science were served up to him, he cried, like St Augustine, 'And these were the dishes in which they brought to me, being hungry, the Sun and Moon, instead of Thee.'   *Desmond MacCarthy on Ruskin*

I could not persuade the Germans of the possibility that a knowledge of liquid hydrogen did not entitle one to judgements upon how a civil servant should be chosen.   *H. J. Laski*

It is only our scientists now who suppose that their opinions on subjects outside their own competence are of importance. The illusion will pass.   *Harold Nicolson*

In memoriam Josephi Thomson, qui, propter minimarum particularum scientiam maximo utriusque universitatis collegio praepositus, alteram officii partem omnino neglexit, altera ita functus est ut neglectam maluisses. Raucus, edentulus, impexus, uxorem duxit non amabilem, cujus ope et auxilio suffultus, heredibus LXXX milia librarum sterling-arum, collegio domicilium hara immundius, posteris exemplum memorablile avaritiae reliquit.

 [In memory of Joseph Thomson who, by virtue of his knowledge of the smallest particles, attained the Mastership of the greatest college in either university. He totally negected the one part of his duties and discharged the other in such a way that it would have been better if he had neglected that also. Loud-mouthed, toothless and unkempt, he married an unpleasant wife, thanks to whose money he was able to leave eighty thousand pounds sterling to his heirs, a house filthier than a pig-stye to the college, and to posterity a model of avarice never to be forgotten.]

 A. S. F. Gow on Sir Joseph Thomson, once Master of Trinity

The road to Hell is paved with good inventions.　　*F. L. Lucas*

For an ague, make six middling pills of cobwebs. A cut: bind on toasted cheese. Stomach ache (the iliac passion) : hold a live puppy constantly on the belly.
　　John Wesley: Primitive Physic (36 editions, 1747–1840)

Dropsy began to threaten, but seasonable physic stopped the inundation.　　*Johnson in a letter*

The famous doctor Boerhaave had an ulcer on his thigh when he was twelve years old. It went on for five years; then he cured it himself 'by tormenting the part with salt and urine.'
　　Boswell's Life of Johnson

Tennyson said that at his school there was one boy kind to him, he became a horse stealer; one bully, who became a 'beloved physician'.

Report from Medical Officer, Holloway Gaol. 'Mrs Ellis was in good health, and in a fit state of health for execution.'

An immense amount of drivel all the more tiresome since the futility of superstition is linked to the dullness of science.
　　Hensley Henson on psychoanalysis (after reading it up)

science

This much vaunted psychoanalysis is mainly nonsense. Certainly nothing could be more contemptible than the blethering of Freud on the subject of dreams.   *Hensley Henson*

Though Sigmund Freud is sure of a place in history, opinion may be divided as to whether he was a great scientist or just a dirty old man. Either view could be supported by careful selection of the material in the letters he wrote to Wilhelm Fliess over the turn of the century. (The other half of the correspondence is not available—Freud destroyed it, and wished also to destroy his own share but was not permitted to do so—and we know little of his correspondent except that his special study was 'the relations between the nose and the female sex organs', a subject which enabled him to live in affluence in private practice in Berlin.)

The Origins of Psycho-Analysis : Letters to Wilhelm Fliess,
Drafts and Notes, 1887–1902 by Sigmund Freud. TLS

One of Freud's disciples (Stekel) broke with him, saying that a dwarf on a giant's shoulders saw further than the giant. Freud replied that this does not apply to a louse on the head of an astronomer.

～

STATES OF MIND

Make it an invariable and obligatory law to yourself never to mention your own mental diseases; if you are never to speak of them you will think on them but little, and if you think little of them they will molest you rarely. When you talk of them, it is plain that you want either praise or pity; for praise there is no room, and pity will do you no good; therefore, from this hour speak no more, think no more, about them.

Johnson on hypochondria (to Boswell, 8 April 1780)

The lowest pitch . . . an acquiescence in discouragement which reaches the utmost of sadness when it ceases to be regretful.

Francis Paget on Accidie

I am i' the way to study a long silence.
To prate were idle. I remember nothing.
There's nothing of so infinite vexation
As man's own thoughts—

Webster

Arrogance is worse than a hundred concubines.

(Erasmus heard Dean Colet say to his clergy)

I look upon you as a man called by sorrow and anguish and a strange desolation of hopes into quietness and a soul set apart and made peculiar to God.   *Coleridge to Lamb*

Sophistication is a state of mind which consists in knowing too much of the periphery of life, too little of the core and centre—a sort of cosmic equivalent of wisdom—terrifying to the uninitiated.   *Alston*

The pleasantest dotage that I ever read, saith Laurentius, was of a gentleman at Senes in Italy who was afraid to p——, lest all the towne should be drowned. The physician caused the bells to be rung backward, and told him the towne was on fire, whereupon he made water, and was immediately cured.'

Burton on delusion, from 'The Anatomy of Melancholy'

From the womb to the grave we are never thoroughly awake.

Donne

states of mind

In an asylum ward a man just on his way out, cured, suddenly gave the matron a terrific kick and afterwards said God had distinctly ordered him to do it. Whereupon an elderly white-bearded man shouted: 'You're a liar, I never gave any orders of the kind.' *H. Belloc*

Fanaticism consists of redoubling your effort when you have forgotten your aim. *Santayana*

Jesus and Shelley and Whitman . . . stedfast in faith, never wavering. *Lionel Johnson at Winchester*

The Corps Commander's ADC bought at the fun shop a *pot de chambre* which, on being lifted, played a tune. It was supposed to put visiting generals at their ease.

Peter the Great was tortured by night-fears. If no wife or mistress was available he took an orderly to bed with him and pillowed his head on the man's stomach. If the man moved or snored or had internal regurgitations, he was soundly flogged when morning came. *Harold Nicolson*

A lady . . . felt a thud upon her bed . . . and hands constantly moving over it. She was so frightened that she fainted. When she came to it was daylight and she found that the butler had walked in his sleep and had laid the table for fourteen upon her bed. *Augustus Hare : The Story of my Life*

It is by the acceptation of the traditional and the formal that we escape from the fretful. This was never very far from Pater's mind.

George Moore

Things seem to be going fairly well now that a spirit of pessimism prevails in all departments.

Charles W. Eliot, President of Harvard

He heightened all his sins
Saw Helen in a harlot
Even his pink gins
Were scarlet.

F. Singleton : 'The Optimist'

Optimism and pessimism are moods which reveal nothing except the temperament of the writer. *Dean Inge*

The world has always had the same bankrupt look as to us—as of a failed world just re-collecting its old withered forces to begin again and do better.

Emerson (tonic for ageing pessimists)

'I do not promise overmuch,
Child; overmuch;
Just neutral-tinted haps and such.'

Thomas Hardy

states of mind

The mind must have some worldly objects to excite its attention, otherwise it will stagnate in indolence, sink in melancholy, or rise into visions and enthusiasm.

Johnson

The running winds of Springtime call
For culmination and repose,
And Autumn, letting roses fall,
Sighs for the Spring that brings the rose.

O searching hands and questing feet,
And love and longing still denied,
There is not any hour complete,
Nor any season satisfied.

Gerald Gould

To be uncertain is to be uncomfortable, but to be certain is to be ridiculous.

Goethe

Greek sayings [1] (see page from GWL's manuscript opposite)

---

[1] The first, the quatrain, is not by Menander, according to The Oxford Book of Greek Verse, but is from a poem by Aesopus (c. 400 A.D.?) called 'The Way of Life'. It starts: 'How could anyone cope with you, Life, without being dead? You are full of such untold miseries; and it isn't easy to avoid them, let alone bear them.' Then it goes on as per GWL : 'The nice things about you are the things which are lovely in themselves: the earth, the sea, the stars, the circlings of the moon, and of the sun. All the rest is fear and pain. And if anything good does come anyone's way he gets something very bad in exchange [i.e. Nemesis].

The next three come from Aeschylus's 'Prometheus'.

1. All things are a burden unless you reign with the gods.
2. Cleverness loses out to necessity in the long run.
3. Time ages us and teaches us all the lessons.
4. [From Homer]. Of all that breathes and moves upon earth, nothing is more pitiable than man.

Gould. "The running winds of springtime call
For culmination and repose.
And Autumn, letting roses fall,
Sighs for the spring that brings the rose.

O searching hands and questing feet,
And love and longing still denied,
There is not any hour complete,
Nor any reason satisfied.
                                        Gerald Gould.

God. "helping god to a victory over his own by-products & nonentity"
                                        Olw. Holmes.
Goethe
To be uncertain is to be uncomfortable, but to be certain is to be
    ridiculous "   Goethe

Greek sayings
    ἥδεα μὲν γάρ σου τὰ φύσει καλά, γαῖα θάλασσα,
        ἄστρα σεληναίης κύκλα, καὶ ἠελίου·
    τἄλλα δὲ πάντα φόβοι τε καὶ ἄλγεα κἤν τι πάθῃ τις
        ἐσθλόν, ἀμοιβαίην ἐκδέχεται Νέμεσιν.   Menander

"   ἅπαντ' ἐπαχθῆ πλὴν θεοῖσι κοιρανεῖν

"   Τέχνη δ' ἀνάγκης ἀσθενεστέρα μακρῷ

"   ἀλλ' ἐκδιδάσκει πάνθ' ὁ γηράσκων Χρόνος.

"   οὐ μὲν γάρ τι πού ἐστιν ὀιζυρώτερον ἀνδρὸς,
    πάντων ὅσσα τε γαῖαν ἔπι πνείει τε καὶ ἕρπει.

A page from the Commonplace Book (reduced)

Next week looks very black—a pleasure for every day.

Darwins (one of them)

Now that sin is old-fashioned as Moses
Don't be hard on your neighbour's neuroses.
When he murders for pelf, keep reminding yourself
That we all have our little psychoses.

Author unknown

Our stability is but balance, and wisdom lies
In masterful administration of the unforeseen.

R. Bridges

In general, the greatest reverses of fortune are the most easily borne from a sort of dignity belonging to them.   *Hazlitt*

Stretcht out to all things, and with all content.   *Traherne*

~

STYLE

Ce qui distingue les grands génies, c'est la généralisation et la création . . . Est-ce qu'on ne croit pas à l'existence de Don Quichotte comme à celle de César? Shakespeare . . . ce n'était pas un homme mais un continent; il y avait des grands hommes en lui, des foules entières, des paysages. Ils n'ont pas besoin de faire du style, ceux-là; ils sont forts en dépit de toutes leurs fautes et à cause d'elles. Mais nous, les petits, nous ne valons que par l'exécution achevée . . . Je hasarde ici une proposition que je n'oserais dire nulle part: c'est que les très grands hommes écrivent souvent fort mal, et tant mieux pour eux. Ce n'est pas là qu'il faut chercher l'art de la forme, mais chez les seconds (Horace, La Bruyère, etc).   *Flaubert*

Style, often best with the uneducated, e.g. Hardy's milkman. 'A good saying, well spit out, is a Christmas fire to my withered heart.'

A simple style is like a white light. It is complex but does not seem so. *Desmond MacCarthy*

Ten year-old child's response to 'Describe a bird and a beast'.
The bird that I am going to write about is the owl. The owl cannot see at all by day and at night is as blind as a bat.

I do not know much about the owl so I will go on to the beast which I am going to choose. It is the cow. The cow is a mammal. It has 6 sides—right, left, an upper and below. At the back it has a tail on which hangs a brush. With this it sends the flies away so that they do not fall into the milk. The head is for the purpose of growing horns and so that the mouth can be somewhere. The horns are to butt with, and the mouth is to moo with. Under the cow hangs the milk. It is arranged for milking. How the cow does it I have not yet realised, but it makes more and more. The cow has a fine sense of smell. One can smell it far away. This is the reason for the fresh air in the country.

The man cow is called an ox. It is not a mammal. The cow doesn't eat much, but what it eats it eats twice so that it gets enough. When it is hungry it moos, and when it says nothing it is because its inside is all full up with grass.
Sir Ernest Gowers: The Complete Plain Words

Le style est comme le bonheur; il vient de la douceur de l'âme.
Buffon

Caressez longtemps votre phrase, elle finira par sourire.
Anatole France

style

Men began to hunt more after words than matter, more after the choiceness of the phrase, and the round clean composition of the sentence, and the sweet falling of the clauses, and the varying and illustration of their works with tropes and figures, than after the weight of matter, worth of subject, soundness of argument, life of invention or depth of judgement.

Bacon : The Advancement of Learning. (Anti-Ciceronian)

Words are but the lackeys of Reason, of which to send more than will perform the business is superfluous. The virtue of things is not in their bigness but in their quality, and so of Reason, which, wrapped in a few words, hath the best tang.

Sir W. Cornwallis, 17th cent.

I hate false words, and seek with difficulty and moroseness those that fit the thing. *Landor*

Les mots pompeux ne sont souvent que l'homage que les illettrés rendent au dieu inconnu, le style. *M. Heyguet*

Ce n'est qu'en cherchant les mots qu'on trouve les pensées.

Joubert

It is not pathetic messages that make us shed tears, but the miracle of a word in the right place. *Cocteau*

The minute a phrase becomes current it becomes an apology for not thinking to the end of the sentence.

O. W. Holmes

There was nobody in whose company one felt so much of the

ineffable comfort of being quite safe against an attack of platitude.   *John Morley on Mark Pattison*

To write well without humour is the supreme test. Humour is but a crutch, by the aid of which almost any writer can totter a little way.   *George Moore*

In the end the voices are reducible to two: that in which we dispute and assert, and the other in which we 'whisper conclusions to one another'—the polemical, expository, forensic, homiletic; and the dialectic . . . The men of Charles II's time were the first generation to think of themselves as Modern; they needed a prose to match . . . hence Dryden, Addison, Swift, etc.
G. M. Young

Must we all write and talk a kind of Basic Slang English, and abjure all buns from which the currants have not been extracted?
G. M. Young, against Dobrée, Maugham, Murry, etc.

A mare will eat oats and a hare will eat oats, and a kid will eat ivy too.   *Walter de la Mare on rhythm*

So the mower mows. Every sweep of his scythe varies slightly in its rhythmical circuities. Step by step he fells the flowering weeds and grasses, singing and dappling bird and butterfly overhead and the faint airs of summer, and at length the now patterned meadow is completely mown.   *Id.*

All right to end a sentence with a preposition—but not a paragraph. That should end with the blow of an axe.
O. W. Holmes

⁓

One of Nelson's officers saw a man praying beside his gun just before Trafalgar, and asked him if he was afraid. 'Afraid,' said the man contemptuously. 'No; I was only praying that the enemy's shot may be distributed in the same proportion as the prize money, the greatest part among the officers.'

Percy : 'Anecdotes of War'

War provokes pillage, Pillage brings ruin,
Ruin brings patience, Patience implies peace.
Peace provokes abudance, Abundance brings riches,
Riches bring arrogance, Arrogance brings war,
Thus does peace produce war.

Written on wall of shelled house, France (1917)

No one can predict, no one can even imagine how this terrible war against German and Nazi aggression will run its course, how far it will spread, or how long it will last. Long dark months of trials and tribulations lie before us. Not only great dangers, but many more misfortunes, many shortcomings, many mistakes, many disappointments will surely be our lot. Death and sorrow will be the companions of our journey, hardship our garment, constancy and valour our only shield. We must be united, we must be undaunted, we must be inflexible. Our qualities and deeds must burn and glow through the gloom of Europe until they become the veritable beacon of its salvation.

Winston Churchill

Injurious time, now with a robber's haste
Crams his rich thievery up, he knows not how;
As many farewells as be stars in heaven,
With distinct breath and consign'd kisses to them,
He fumbles up into a loose adieu;

And scants us with a single famish'd kiss,
Distasted with the salt of broken tears.

War-time parting perfectly described (according to Ivor Brown) in 'Troilus and Cressida'

~

Madam Cresswell, a notorious procuress (1670) left £10 to a preacher to preach a sermon at her funeral on condition that he was to say nothing but well of her. One was found who, after generalising on morality, told the congregation of this will and added 'She was born well, she lived well and she died well, for she was born a Cresswell, she lived in Clerkenwell, and she died in Bridewell.'

'I am J.W.C. I do what I please;
They ask for an ice-house, I'll give them a frieze.'
Athenaeum Club. Frieze suggested by Croker.
Keynote of Club: silence and frigidity

A woman (Mrs Brooke) was always worrying Dr Johnson to look through her tragedy (*Siege of Sinope*). He kept her at bay and advised her to look it over herself. She said she had no time— 'too many irons in the fire'. Johnson, out of patience at last, said 'the best thing I can advise you to do is to put your tragedy along with your irons.' *Hannah More*

Thomas, J. H. on a colleague: ' 'E don't carry much ice.'
Edward Marsh: 'No, nor cut many guns.'

George Robins, famous auctioneer, described a gallows as 'picturesque hanging wood'.

Young man in restaurant tried to catch young lady's eye—failed, and being annoyed said as he passed her, 'I am sorry I tried to catch your attention but I mistook you for my mother.' Young lady: 'Then I suppose you never noticed I was wearing a wedding-ring.'   *E. S. P. Haynes*

Dorothy Parker, when President Coolidge's death was announced. 'But how do they know?'

> Whose love is given over-well
> Shall look on Helen's face in Hell,
> Whilst they whose love is thin and wise
> May view John Knox in paradise
> *Dorothy Parker : 'Partial Comfort'*

He didn't believe a thought was deep because it was a bit thick.
                    H. M. Tomlinson on Robert Lynd

We have lost a lot of popularity in my time because there are not two sides to as many questions as we think.   *Vansittart*

A wit said to A. Bennett that the hideous marble in the Holborn Restaurant grill room (called the Gorgonzola) was really a picture of a great battle in which the Gorgons overthrew the Zola system.

Madoc by Southey, Porson said, would be remembered when Homer and Virgil are forgotten—but not before.

Buchan on Scott says 'Scott's worldliness has nothing of what we call snobbery.' H. Kingsmill comments: 'This is a certificate of Falstaff's solvency issued by Mr Micawber.'

Wit is so shining a quality that everybody admires it, most people aim at it, all people fear it, and few love it except in themselves. *Chesterfield*

~

WOMEN

> She smiled like a holy day
> And simpred like the Spring
> She pranck't it like a popingaie
> And like a swallow sing,
> She trip't it like a barren doe
> She strutted like a gor-crowe.
> Which made the men so fond of her
> Hye nonny nonny noe.
> > *From an anonymous poem of circa 1640,*
> > *beginning 'Sweet she was, as kind a love*
> > *As ever fettered swayne'*

Unless a woman has amorous heat she is a dull companion, and to have amorous heat in elegant perfection the fancy should be warmed with lively ideas. *Johnson : Life of Prior*

Lady Dillon told Sir F. Chantrey that English women were more buxom than Italian women. The delicate way she put it was, 'you will find that Italian women can sit much closer to a wall than English.'

> *Stanhope: Conversations with the Duke of Wellington*

Dear Sir, I enclose a cheque for 22/6 for the payment of a dog-licence for three years. You may say I have no dog; that is true. You may insist that I never had a dog. But I have a wife who is such a bitch that I feel morally obliged to accept the responsibilities of my position. Yours faithfully.

Conscience money

I think on the whole much better of women than of men, but I do not tell it to them. They have far more courage; they face disease and death better than we do, they have more pity and less vanity. Their instinct is on the whole a safer guide through their life than our intelligence; they do not make fools of themselves as often as we do (though it is perhaps true that a really foolish woman reaches a lower depth than a similar man).

Axel Munthe

Arsène Houssaye, director of the Théatre Français, asked Mlle George about Napoleon whose mistress she had been. 'Is it true he sent for you long after midnight and forgot you were there until morning, absorbed as he was in the map of Europe?' 'Pure slander', she replied with dignity. 'he knew what was due to me and what was due to himself . . . His map of Europe ! *I* was his map of Europe.'

Cambridge lecturer about island where there is a great preponderance of men said, 'Even Newnhamites could find a husband.' The Newnhamites left as protest. 'No hurry, the boat doesn't go till Friday.'

All the women who ever wrote original stuff could have been strangled at birth and the history of English literature (and my bookshelves) would be unchanged. *T. E. Lawrence*

She had a great soul and a perfectly enormous bottom.

Sainte-Beuve on George Sand

She became a legend in her old age, but of that I have nothing to say, for we did not meet, and except for a few broken letters did not write, and she was never old to me. Let those who may complain that it was all on paper, remember that only on paper has humanity yet achieved glory, beauty, truth, knowledge, virtue and abiding love.

G. B. Shaw on Ellen Terry

It begins with a thrill like that of a hot bath, delicious. But we desire a deeper intensity, and there comes a feeling of melting, as if all the knots were loosening, and this is followed by a tearing, till soul and body are about to part. We know not whether it be pain or pleasure . . . A moment comes of madness so acute that we feel we cannot live through it. We do somehow. Afterwards the blood weighs heavy as if it were lead, and then comes long voluptuousness, the brain is overwhelmed in it; a throbbing ecstasy and pulsing beat.

Communicated to George Moore by a woman

Edward Thomas saw outside a fried-fish shop 'Cleanliness, economy, and civility, always hot and always ready' and remarked 'the motto of the perfect wife.'

E. S. P. Haynes

Samuel Baldwin insisted on being buried at sea because his wife had often told him that when he was dead she would dance on his grave.

~

APPENDICES

APPENDIX I

Charles Fisher

by

G.W.L.

Charles Fisher

CHARLES FISHER

IT is very difficult to write even an adequate sketch of Charles. My mind wanders back over a dozen years and gathers up a harvest of delightful recollections, but the attempt to produce them finds the ink dry on the pen and the paper blank. It is a commonplace observation, but peculiarly true of Charles, that no record of his talk and his doings can possibly shew what he really was. All who ever knew him realised the truth of the poet's words:

For never, of all his nurslings yet, was Great Tom tolled

For one more manly modelled or more princely souled.

Yet when I write about him I call to mind little but what is fugitive and trivial—faded little incidents of fun and companionship, which drew all their colour and freshness from his overflowing humanity and great laughter.

It was nearly always in the holiday time that we met, and no one enjoyed a holiday like Charles; we talked of many things, but, as with Dr Johnson's friend who failed to acquire philosophy, somehow 'Cheerfulness was always breaking in.' One ought, no doubt, to remember long conversations from which emerged his definite views on important subjects, but such was not his way. Abundant comment there was, trenchant and illuminating, but he rarely embarked on discussion and gave the impression of being rather impatient of it. His own opinions were not the outcome of discussion but of his own observation, nor did he much desire to exchange them. He was rather antagonistic to those earnest and courageous souls who attempted with too heavy a hand to draw him into the open. With a kind of Olympian aloofness he would repel a too intimate intrusion, and, not from want of sympathy but from his own very strong and sensitive feeling for independence, he shewed no desire to convert or convince. It was said of the Irishman Synge that, if you talked to him of Home Rule, he yawned; what he really wanted to know was what the coster said to the policeman. So with Charles. He did not care a straw what anyone's externals were, their class or profession or opinions, but went straight for the human core of each individual, only baffled by bigotry and pretentiousness and pachydermous conventionality, and that is why a muster of his firm friends would include exquisites and business men, athletes and recluses, mystics and pagans, poets and philistines, besides servants and shopkeepers and gardeners and cabmen.

His Open Sesame to all hearts was his humour, using the word in its widest sense. No situation or human being was impervious to it. Besides the ordinary connotations of humour, a sense of the ludicrous and verbal felicity, both of which he had in full, the basis of it was an immense appreciation of the under currents of character and situation, all that which 'needs a nail scratch 'ere 'tis laid you bare.' He would seize upon and draw out what was individual or incongruous and expand it into delicious absurdity, with a lightness of touch and a kind of large kindliness that made him irresistible. He did not make fun of these peculiarities, he delighted in them; and the victim, submerged in titanic laughter, had no choice but to laugh too, conscious, however, all the time of the delight rather than the mockery.

Charles first came to my home, Hagley, in 1902. He came so often afterwards that the innumerable incidents of which he is the centre are inextricably mixed, but I remember we noticed at once, as no one could help noticing, his enormous pleasure in common things—sun and wind, the feel of grass to the feet and rain on the face, cold water, alfresco games,—which made him the perfect companion.

He was very soon completely at home at Hagley, and became as one of the family. His visits depended on no set invitation given or answered; he just appeared, if possible timing his stay to avoid Sunday in well-founded mistrust of his self-control under a country sermon. Hagley is a place which might appear to some to possess considerable drawbacks. The Black Country is close by and sends forth a blight over the land when the wind is in the north, and the rain often falls with pitiless concentration when the wind goes to the south. Charles shared Belloc's opinion that the Midlands are 'sodden and unkind', or at any rate strongly conducive to a depressed and inactive life. He wrote from the 'Invincible' that he wished to do nothing after the War but to go bed for five years, only getting up for meals, adding that this was not to be considered incompatible with an earlier wish to 'end his days in a Worcestershire vicarage, having helped to settle the date of Deuteronomy.' The house itself was built before comfort was much thought of, and has changed little. Unless you were in luck your general impression might be that there was no light, natural or artificial, that the bells didn't ring, nor the clocks go, nor the windows open, nor the taps run. Charles liked it all the better for these eccentricities, which he preferred to regard as a completely suitable setting for the occupants.

He strongly disapproved of any change, especially in the direction of comfort, even if it was only a new wall-paper in the bathroom; and to the last he used the original rain-water tap which filled the bath with a rank liquid, coloured by the Dudley flues. He always insisted on having the same room, giving as his reason his fondness for the works of Bishop Pilkington whose volumes line the walls immediately outside. A further reason alleged was that his night's rest was only assured if he knew that no sound louder than the cough of a Worcestershire sheep could come and disturb it. In the hall downstairs there are numerous plaster casts of well-known Greek statuary, which were parodied by Charles with such merciless felicity that their original characters have vanished, and to none of us will Hermes ever recall anything but the bowler-hatted umpire with the bails, and in place of Bacchus we shall only see 'Warner from his bath declaring the innings closed.'

He at once made firm friends with everyone from my Father—to whom Charles with affectionate irreverence gave the name of Chob, later in common though clandestine use—

down to my sister Nan's infant John, who saw with the unerring instinct of three years that here was the last word in bears, horses, tunnels or playmates in general. Chob's vein of cheerful pessimism in comment or prophecy concerning the prospects of himself, his family, and his friends had a special appeal for Charles, and he was untiring in his manœuvres to acquire and store up examples of it, hailing his frequent successes with open hilarity. Their relations remained undisturbed by the discovery announced at an early stage in the friendship by Chob. 'Charles I believe, regards me as a person of great singularity and is always on the lookout for manifestations of it.' Charles would always seek out Chob's company at Lord's, and, when allowed by the hostess, at the Hagley dinner table, after which he would triumphantly declare that Chob was 'no older and as good company as ever.' My father on his part was frequently heard to ask whether Fisher (Christian names are a modern growth) was not coming soon; a question not often asked about a guest over 30 years younger than himself.

The diverse interests of the rest of the family Charles followed with humorous solicitude, and invested them all with a thick atmosphere of nonsense so that the effect was produced that each of us was gravely playing a part solely for his benefit as audience. Dick's excursions into scienctific and practical agriculture, under the twin auspices of Professor Biffen at Cambridge and the Hagley cowman, were pictured as heroic effort doomed to failure by fate and incompetence. When Dick's telephone wire in France was trodden on by a cow, Charles wrote 'I hope Dick punished the cow by milking it.' Caryl was assumed to be shaping his life and thought with a view to becoming Bishop of Stourbridge; Rachel and I were engaged in praiseworthy attempts to gild hopelessly bucolic tastes with a veneer of culture: Rachel, through a medium of Beethoven and Swift, while I was never allowed to escape the consequences of an admission that I found William Watson a better poet than T. E. Brown.

It was at Hagley, I believe, that Charles learnt to play golf; the sight of him on the links is very vivid. He was a scandalous golfer for one of his natural advantages. He hated all the paraphernalia of the game, the caddies, the etiquette, the solemn jargon, and made a point of ignoring it all. I can see him striding to the first tee, pockets stuffed with re-made, re-painted, second- or possibly third-hand balls, all doomed to early oblivion in gorse, pool or wood. He preferred no caddie, but if one was forced on him, a bag of heterogeneous instruments, few and rusty, was handed over, Charles watching closely for signs of surprise or derision on the boy's face. Then the drive off—a lurch of the great shoulders comprising all known golfing errors, followed by a wholly problematic flight on the part of the ball. A favourite shot of his was a far-travelling scurry at right angles to the proper line. 'It's all right Georgie, I've opened up the hole for you,' was the shattering euphemism employed on such occasions. Similarly, 'I know the shot you like,' braced his partner to prepare for a desperate brassie shot from long grass instead of the expected easy approach. A complacent murmur of 'Poetry' signalised the rare co-operation of hand and eye, perfect flight and direction. He would always play in a foursome if he possibly could, as providing more company and few opportunities of exposure; if there were any odds he would be much intrigued with the manipulation of the bisques of his own side, or in attempting by unceasing bluff and gibe to stampede his opponents into the misuse of theirs. I do not think he ever improved much. Once, in response to my inquiry after his progress at Hayling Island, the oracular answer came: 'The Committee have their eye on me,' but whether with a view to honorary membership or suspension I never found out. He could no doubt have been a good player, but he disliked rules and dogma in all things, especially in games; and golf, unless begun in the nursery, is exacting in this respect. It is impossible to picture Charles, text-book in hand, eradicating his faults in a lonely corner of the links!

His keenness to win games was much less than his enjoyment of them, which was immense. But he saw through them
and over them and knew exactly their place and value. He
was at all times a great walker. One of the best times I ever
had with him was a week at the Lakes. We set out from Hagley,
greatly stimulated by Chob's tragic forebodings. Charles maintained that the gist of Chob's parting advice as to his recently
sprained ankle was that though hill-climbing was obviously
dangerous, a still nastier wrench attended a fall on the level,
while most disastrous, because most unexpected, was to turn
your ankle while standing still, but that I suspect was *ben
trovato*. The lakes were at their best. The inns were empty
and we had samples of every kind of weather on a background
of searching rain. Charles was thoroughly characteristic. He
refused to take more forethought than is required for a walk
to church. He scoffed at any suggeston of a ruck-sack or such
like. 'We're not going into the wilderness; hot water laid on at
every corner.' He had no stick, no nails in his shoes (Burberry
slip-ons, as Caryl called them, going off and on without
unlacing), and an ordinary suit of the familiar blue flannel.
He paid no attention to the map. He seized it from me from
time to time, but merely in order to acquire a few more melo-
dious and mouth-filling names to roll off his tongue. That
done, the map would be handed back crumpled, sodden with
rain, wrong section uppermost, without having told Charles
where we were or which way our course led. 'Keep to the
high ground then we can't go wrong,' was his reiterated conviction which experience was powerless to shatter, and his
profound content so long as he was under the winds and open
sky was infectious enough to obliterate all the importance of
such things as rest and regular meals. But he was very suspi-
cious of 'under-catering', and the morning visit to the village
shop to lay in provisions for the day was not lightly treated.

The other piece of daily ritual was the despatching of half-
a-dozen postcards to various friends; many will remember
these cryptic communications, of such character with all their

terseness that getting one was like a lightening glimpse of
Charles himself. Sometimes it might be a telegram, especially
when careful timing would point the jest. I cannot resist giving an instance. Once at Cambridge there was an athletic meeting between the University team and the Racing Club of
France. I was to put the weight against one Parouskovopoulos.
At the height of the proceedings they were interrupted by
the arrival of a telegram for me bearing the pathetic appeal
'Have mercy on my boy' signed 'Parouskovopoulos père.' The
Oxford stamp betrayed the perpetrator, but in any case no
one but Charles would have instinctively divined that 'My
boy' was fifty years old and nineteen stone in weight.

The only other thing Charles was at all particular about
was the choice of books, one apiece to read in the evening,
Jacobi being impossible. He brought 'Carnival', mainly on the
grounds that he saw no chance of finishing it unless he had
no other with him. I was merely obvious and brought a Wordsworth, but Charles read it most of the time, and 'Carnival'
was not only never finished but was left behind to shock Canon
Rawnsley. Charles would produce Wordsworthian fragments
at frequent intervals in a walk, much as De Quincey for days
together used to repeat the words 'And Belshazzar the King
made a great feast to a thousand of his lords' just for the pleasure of their sound. I remember one or two fragments.

> So have I, not unmoved in mind,
> Seen birds of tempest-loving kind
> Thus beating up against the wind.

was a favourite. Also some resounding lines from 'To Joanna'
telling of Hammer-Scar of Loughrigg and Glaramara and
Silver-How and an imperial stanza of Matthew Arnold's which
I had not seen or heard quoted by anyone else:

> Thin, thin, the pleasant human noises grow,
> And faint the city gleams;
> Rare the lone pastoral huts—marvel not thou;
> The solemn peaks but to the stars are known,
> But to the stars and the cold lunar beams;

Alone the sun arises, and alone
Spring the great streams.

But this was his limit as regards length. How he would have
hated to think there was any danger of his being pictured as
a spouter of poetry from mountain tops!

He had a very fine taste in poetry, with a ruthless eye for
what was hollow or precious, and a most contemptuous snort
for anything that savoured of 'chatter about Harriet.' I remember an illuminating observation which summed up his
attitude. 'You can see how the good things are written, but
when you get the real stuff you can only wonder how the
devil he did it.' This was actually said of 'La Belle Dame sans
Merci.' He also said once that in the honours list of poetry he
would put 'Lycidas' and 'Adonais' bracketed first. It is perhaps unfair to record these passing judgements, but it seems
to me they need not shrink from challenge. His classical and
literary achievements can be more properly dealt with by those
who were in closer touch with his work. All I ever saw of him
in working hours was in the periodical visit he paid to Eton to
examine in the Entrance Scholarships, but that was, of course,
a mere holiday-task. According to his own account, the only
hard work in it was to defeat the candidates who had come
from schools which he suspected of cramming tendencies,
and that he generally failed to do. He always used to occupy
our spare bedroom, from which there was a magnificent view
over the roofs of Eton up to the majestic profile of Windsor
Castle. Charles, as was his way, wove a web of romance over
the proximity of the Castle, and saw the influence of royalty
in many daily phenomena. When late for breakfast, he would
plead that loyalty forbade him to rise before the King had put
a leg out of bed, for which he watched from his pillow. A
sudden peal from some distant belfry was the King ringing
for his boots, and the noisy escape of steam from a South-
Western Engine drew a sympathetic reference to His Majesty's asthma.

He had many firm friends at Eton through Oxford and cricket and scholarship. In the 'Invincible' he used to enjoy getting occasional classical effusions from members of the staff, which he would roll out in the night watches to the searching test of the winds and the waves. He was fond of Eton, and, on the whole, appreciative of its product, though complaining, as he did once at Bamburgh, that the cry of the Old Etonian in Tom Quad was a poor exchange for that of the sea-bird. The last letter I had from him expressed the hope to be examining at Eton again as soon as he had renewed his acquaintance with the construction of $\pi\rho\acute{\iota}\nu$ and *quippe qui.*

Among other things he looked forward to, from the monotonous strain of the sea, were: 'to wear a bowler hat again; to lie in bed of a morning with no routine before him; and never again to watch the sun rise.' Well, this last wish is fulfilled, and like Synge's Michael, he has 'a clean burial in the far North.' To say he is one of those who will never stop being missed means at the same time everything and nothing. When peace comes again and holiday pursuits are once more possible, many of us will look round for the perfect friend and not find him, but at the same time his memory is and will be more vivid than the presence of most others.

Charles' friendship was a gift from the gods. He came like a great wind into the life of his friends, sweeping away all cobwebs and scattering joy and health and sanity. He urged no precepts, argued no cause, preached no doctrine; merely by his love of great and simple things and his impetuous gaiety of heart, he bore irresistible witness to the value of life and the heroic essence of man.

We who knew him required no hero's end to prove his high lineage, but there is nevertheless a crowning splendour about that last evening of May which silences the tongue by its complete and final fitness, and almost satisfies the heart with its clear message that, as in life so in his death, there was nothing but well and fair.

January 1917

APPENDIX II

Correspondence between
Rupert Hart-Davis and George Lyttelton,
pre-1955 (before the *Lyttelton Hart-Davis Letters*)

NOTE

Twenty-eight letters (including postcards) are printed here. Rupert Hart-Davis's first letter is missing. He dictated all the others in the office in the course of his busy publishing day. Carbon copies were kept even of the briefest notes. George Lyttelton's replies from Suffolk are handwritten and one, as indicated on p. 157, is missing.

Editing has been kept to a minimum.

14 February 1949   *Finndale House*
                                        Grundisburgh
                                             Suffolk

Dear Rupert Hart-Davis,

I remember you very well—and your recitation of 'Love in the Valley'.[1] All the most distinguished men of this generation seem to have been in that Extra Studies division, beginning with J. B. S. Haldane and Aldous Huxley. I am well aware that I am exactly resembling the fly on the chariot-wheel who exclaimed 'What a dust I do raise!', but no one ever grudged the poor thing its complacency, so I continue to reminisce on this high note!

I agree with you *entirely* about N. Cardus[2], and will at once start exploring avenues and pulling strings. Nothing may come of it, for I will not conceal from you that the MCC committee, if it has a fault, is perhaps a little fixed in its ways and has the customary terror of such bodies of 'setting up a precedent'. But I will see what can be done without delay. As Mr Squeers said of himself, 'You have come to the right shop for morals', so you could not find anyone who has a higher opinion of N.C.'s writing than I. No other writer on the game can hold a candle to him. At his best—and how rarely he is not at his best—he is alone and supreme. Of course he ought to have been made a member years ago, however long the queue that had to be jumped. But I must warn you that the literary flair of the Committee is not very sensitive, and that there are odd little streaks of jealousy and exclusiveness, and (let us be frank) snobbery among old cricketers, all of which may stand in his way. But I will do what I can and let you know how I get on.

                                   Yours sincerely,
                                   GEORGE LYTTELTON

1. By George Meredith.
2. Journalist, writer on cricket and music.

137

30 June 1950   *36 Soho Square, London W1*

Dear George Lyttelton,

Here are the two books I promised to send.[1] I greatly look forward to hearing what you think of them.

It was a very special pleasure meeting you last night, and I have made Tim promise to bring us together again.

This is a long way off, but I wonder whether it would amuse you to come as my guest to the autumn meeting of the Johnson Club? I dare say you have been to it before. It meets four times a year in the garret in Gough Square (except for the summer meeting which is usually out of London). It is not frightfully exciting, nor is there a great deal to eat or drink, but if it happened to coincide with a time when you were visiting London, there is nothing that I should like better. I don't exactly know when the autumn meeting is, but I expect it will be some time in October.

Don't bother to answer this until you have looked at the books.

    Yours ever gratefully,

    RUPERT HART-DAVIS

1. The Reynard Library *Johnson*, edited by Mona Wilson,
   and E. V. Lucas's *Cricket all his Life*, his cricket writings assembled
   by Rupert Hart-Davis. Both published by R. H.-D. Ltd in 1950.

6 July 1950   *Grundisburgh*

My dear Rupert Hart-Davis,

I took you at your word and delayed answering till I had perused, as the solicitors say, the two books. My impulse was to record at once my pleasure at meeting you again—the first time surely since you were up to me—and my deep gratitude for your generosity. I do it now in all sincerity. I am delighted to have the best of Johnson in so attractive and portable a form. How good the old man is, and how few people realise what humour there is in his writing, e.g. the Soame Jenyns passage, the False Alarm, Sir Richard Blackmore, etc. Our electorate ought to read what he says about them in the F. A., but who in these timorous days will dare to quote it? Something odd has happened in the first paragraph of p. 945 about 'poor Lyttelton'. My 18th cent. copy has 'returned, in a note which I have read, acknowledgements which can never be proper, since they must be paid either for flattery or for justice.' And there are other little discrepancies of no importance. Miss (Mrs?) Mona Wilson must have been using an 18th century edition, as in the Gray extract she has 'Eaton' where my book (Arthur Murphy 1806) has 'Eton'.

I am delighted too to have Lucas's book. It was a very good notion of yours to collect his cricket utterances. He is not as good as N. Cardus at his very best (*me judice*, nobody is) but N.C. *sometimes* over-writes and E.V.L. never. Both are equally steeped in the game's flavours and traditions, its essence, so to speak. N.C. knows a good deal more about its technique. E.V.L.'s real joy is in the old days and players—the Lumpys and Silver Billys etc. down to W.G. (How he would have envied and admired two of N.C.'s happiest little flings, calling W.G. the Dr Johnson of cricket and Sam Woods the Squire Western!)

He will take his place at my bedside with Cardus, *The Irish R.M.*, Boswell (*and* Mona Wilson), Ivor Brown's word books, *Earlham*, and a Jacobs omnibus.

But enough of this. You are a busy man, and 'Criticism disdains to chase a schoolboy (or ex-schoolmaster) to his commonplaces.' How right that old rascal Agate was in saying that Johnson could always supply the final comment on any everyday occurrence.

Yours with much gratitude,
GEORGE LYTTELTON

10 July 1950   *Grundisburgh*

My dear R. H-D,

I am haunted by the suspicion, which is nearly conviction, that I made in my letter to you no reference to your kind invitation to the Johnson Club dinner later this year. Unpardonable! And grossly stupid too, for I should like it above all things. Please forgive my stark insensibility and ascribe it to the ravages of age. I suppose that what I call my mind was wholly occupied by the two books, and one of them shall speak for me, though I suspect that you are the last person who needs reminding 'that sudden fits of inadvertency will surprise vigilance, slight avocations will seduce attention, and casual eclipses of the mind will darken learning.'[1]

Yours very sincerely,
GEORGE LYTTELTON

1. From Dr Johnson's preface to his Dictionary.

11 July 1950   *36 Soho Square*

My dear G.L.

Very many thanks for your two delightful letters. I am so glad that you would like to come to the Johnson Club dinner and I will let you know directly I can discover the date.

When we were preparing the text for the JOHNSON volume we started off by buying a set of Murphy and then getting a reliable scholar to collate it with the various first editions. To our horror, we soon discovered that Murphy's text was wildly inaccurate, often bearing very little relation to the original. The text of 'The Lives of the Poets' we took from the first editions, slightly supplemented by the second and third, as is explained on page 792 of our edition. Each of the sections of our book, as you may have noticed, has a bibliographical note on the verso of the half-title, explaining the origin of the text we have used.

I love to think of the book by your bedside. My old friend Guy Chapman (now Professor of Modern History at Leeds University) to whom I sent a copy, writes of 'the admirable Johnson, sitting beside my bed's head and dipped into for a blinding flash of common-sense before going to sleep.'

Your critical comparison of Cardus and Lucas agrees exactly with my own ideas, but I think E.V.L. was worth resurrecting.

Greatly looking forward to seeing you in the autumn.

Yours ever,
RUPERT HART-DAVIS

28 September 1950   *Grundisburgh*

Dear Rupert Hart-Davis,

What a kind man you are! I am delighted to have the (practically) complete Goldsmith[1]—what was Carlyle's snapshot of him, 'Just an Irish blackguard with twinkling eyes and a great fund of goosery.' Not bad, but he left out that mysteriously perfect style, having perhaps no great eye for such.

Thank you *very* much. I could really say with the Doctor 'This is taking prodigious pains about a man' and hurry from the room in tears. I look forward to drinking his health with you anon.

Yours very sincerely,
GEORGE LYTTELTON

1. The Reynard Library Goldsmith, ed. Richard Garnett (1950).

5 October 1950   *36 Soho Square*

Dear George Lyttelton,

Thank you so much for your charming letter. I have learnt that the Autumn meeting of the Johnson Club will be at Dr Johnson's house, Gough Square, at 7.30 p.m. on Friday 27th October. After dinner Dr. Russell Brain is to read a paper on 'Dr Johnson and the Kangaroo'. I hope this date will be convenient. If so, I shall look forward to seeing you there.

Yours sincerely,
RUPERT HART-DAVIS

6 October 1950   *Grundisburgh*
[POSTCARD]

I hope you don't share the view of a Victorian aunt of mine who held that a postcard except for announcing one's train was little better than an insult. I shall certainly be at Gough Square on Friday Oct. 27. I will go straight there unless you instruct me otherwise, and in what they call morning dress, risking the chance of being treated as the Dr treated the man who took his

chair at the theatre. The kangaroo opens up a wide field of specu-
lation. At the moment the possible connections with the old man
are obscure.

Very many thanks. G.W.L.

6 March 1951   36 Soho Square

Dear George,

Are you going to the Johnson Club luncheon in March 16th?
I don't fancy the change from dinner in the garret to lunch at
Brown's Hotel (particularly since the change has been made so
that the biggest bore in London may attend!), but if you are
going to be there I shall come for the pleasure of seeing you.

Yours ever,
RUPERT

8 March 1951   Grundisburgh

My dear Rupert,

I was going to attend the Johnson dinner at that incongruous hostel but I shall have to cry off, as they have called
an extra-ordinary meeting of a local School Governing Body
of which I am a member. It is the only day on which the
visitor or whatever the good bishop calls himself can attend,
so there it is. Please let us make a point of meeting at the
next dinner whenever it is, and you must tell me who the
greatest bore in London is. We could produce a few from the
Royal Empire Society who would shake him on his throne.
Nor is Ipswich a mean city in respect of that commodity.

There is a whoreson East wind today and the village of
Grundisburgh is a-rustle with flu germs. I have escaped so
far. But I am rather rheumatic. The other day I sat in a doctor's surgery for 1½ hours awaiting my turn among a score
of plebeian (snob!) old women. They were all emetically

frank about their symptoms, most of which I feel sure indicated ailments hitherto unknown to science. My neighbour,
a vast matron, told the company with quiet pride, as one conscious of great achievement but no boaster, that she 'hadn't
kept a thing down' for three days. I furtively crept to another seat as I didn't know whether she had exhausted her
capital, so to speak. The doctor's ephemeral literature mainly
consisted of journals like 'Vogue' and 'Lilliput' of 1945. On
the whole rather a searing experience, as Stevenson said of
his visit to the leper-settlement (perhaps with less exaggera-
tion). I hope you are flourishing. Your publications are well
to the fore among the critics. As they should be.

Yours ever,
GEORGE LYTTELTON

11 April 1952   *Grundisburgh*

My dear Rupert Hart-Davis,

I hope very much you are going to be at the Johnson dinner
on the 23rd. I have missed the last two; it is a tiresome circumstance that the old man's birth and death days both coincide
with a high tide of examination papers that periodically comes
my way, and for some reason that the most exhaustive researches
have failed to reveal, they all have to be marked *ventre-a-terre*
with hardly any intervals for food and sleep. Don't, if you can
help it, leave me to the tender mercies of those old baskets.

I hope that you are prospering as you deserve—all the signs
are that you are. Never has a biography had a better Press than
your *Hugh Walpole*. My copy is ordered, but the Ipswich book-
shop is spiritually and culturally related to Spottiswoode, whose
answer if you asked for a bible was that no, they hadn't it in
stock, but they knew the book and with luck could get it for you.

I only met H.W. once and liked him very much. I wonder if
your book quotes his saying to old Agate, 'But I shan't forgive
Willie (Maugham) for a long time. Dash it all, the beggar had

143

drunk my claret'. That seems to me the remark of a nice man and it shews up exactly what was wrong with what S.M. had done.

Yours ever,

GEORGE LYTTELTON

22 April 1952   *36 Soho Square*

My dear George,

So sorry not to have answered your charming letter before now, but I have been away with influenza and have only just struggled back to work. Alas, I shan't be there to back you up tomorrow. I am sure you are more than capable of holding your own with all the old boys but I hate to miss the opportunity of seeing you. When are you going to be in London next?

Yours ever,

RUPERT

17 November 1952   *36 Soho Square*

Dear George,

Are you by any happy chance planning to attend the Johnson Club dinner on December 11th? If so, I shall go too; if not, probably not. If you are going, could we perhaps have a drink together first? It would be so nice to see you.

Yours ever,

RUPERT

18 November 1952   *Grundisburgh*

Dear Rupert,

No, I can't manage Dec. 11. It comes just in the middle of a period when I am snowed under by Certificate papers, which for some obscure reason always have to be marked against time.

But I am relying on you to attend the spring meeting when I shall be reading a paper, God help us all. For some weeks I could think of no other subject than a trenchant indictment of the Club as exactly the kind of institution on which Johnson would have emptied the vials of his derision, but I decided in the end that that would not do. And I actually go to Cambridge tomorrow to do some mild research in the Library among some 18th century byways. I beseech you to be present in March or April and greet what you suspect to be meant for jokes with bursts of infectious laughter. Memories of the cold and scholarly eye of Dr Chapman[1] mingle indistinguishably—at about 4 a.m.—with the Suffolk sleet-showers.

How immensely well you did that Hugh Walpole book. I ended by liking him very much. What an odd mixture he was, and fundamentally a far better and nicer man than most of his detractors. No doubt there was something irritating about him—not only his vast success. And they will be still more irritated when they find that his time in purgatory will be far shorter than theirs!

I hope you are prospering. I am sure you are, for a very large proportion of the books that all intelligent men want to read are published by you.

Unless, as I sometimes fear, we are a swiftly diminishing band.

Yours ever,
GEORGE LYTTELTON

1. R. W. Chapman, editor of Johnson's Letters.

20 November 1952   *36 Soho Square*

Dear George,

Thanks so much for your delightful letter. I am sorry you won't be there on the 11th, but I shall undoubtedly lead the claque at the spring meeting. I wish you had followed up your original idea and pitched into the club itself. I don't think it will ever be any fun until the cold eye of Chapman, the moronic laughter of old McArthur, and the dismal presence of one or two others have all been removed. I don't much care for the secretary—do you?

I am so glad you approved of the Walpole book. I feel rather lost without it and would like to tackle something else if I could find anything suitable.

Whenever I said that some book was very good but wouldn't sell, old Edward Garnett used to say: 'You forget, my young friend, that there is still in this country a residuum of educated folk.' I suppose that's still true, but, as you say, the residuum is shrinking. How does Hardy put it in that wonderful poem?

'The thinning of our ranks each year

Affords a hint we are nigh undone.'
I quote from a faulty memory and my secretary is longing to go to lunch, so goodbye for now.

Yours ever,

RUPERT

24 November 1952   *Grundisburgh*

[POSTCARD]

'Why, Sir, as to his being a worthy man, you are to remember that a man's worth is not readily apprehended in the casual and frigid contacts of formal correspondence.'

'But, Sir, is he not a very good secretary?'

'Sir, a man who is so indifferent to exactitude or so deficient in elementary observation that he has mis-spelt the name of poor Lyttelton on every communication which he has addressed to him may claim our regard for an hundred merits, but assuredly sectetarial excellence will not be one of them.'

Some day you must tell me the title of that Hardy poem. Your letter heartened me mightily. G.W.L.

25 November 1952   *36 Soho Square*

Dear George,

I was delighted, abashed, but at the same time somewhat baffled by your ingenious postcard. I have looked at the carbon copies of my last two letters to you (of 17th and 20th November) and find that your name is, so far as I know, correctly spelt on both. Perhaps it was the envelopes that were at fault? My secretary is so accustomed to taking the can-back for my mistakes that she automatically holds out this mysterious receptacle as soon as I am charged with any blunder, and it is true to say that I don't usually see the envelopes.

The Hardy lines come from a poem called 'An Ancient to Ancients'. It is one of my favourites, and I only wish I could avoid Early School by reciting it to you!

Yours ever,

RUPERT

26 November 1952   *Grundisburgh*

Good God, my dear Rupert, it wasn't *you* my poor little jeu d'esprit was aimed at! What a fool one is to be cryptic—one of the pedagogue's besetting sins (do you remember F. W. Dobbs?) But you said in your letter that you didn't think a tremendous lot of the Johnson Club secretary, and my card was to indicate my—and the Doctor's!—agreement. Dash it all , *our* correspondence has, I hope, never been 'formal', still less frigid! Nor have you *once* mis-spelt me, which is a rare occurrence.

I am going to read a paper on my ancestor—whom the Dr disliked—undeterred by the discovery that S. C. Roberts wrote on the same subject 25 years ago. The saurian eye of Dr Chapman will be filmed with disapproval. But I can't help that. And I shall be fortified by your genial presence. Bless you.

Yours ever, G.W.L.

28 November 1952   *36 Soho Square*

My dear George,

What a relief! It was very stupid of me to miss the clue about 'secretaryship' etc., but I dictate so many letters here every day that I cannot always remember what I have said, and I had quite forgotten my remarks about this particular chap. Next time you must illustrate your jokes with diagrams and funny drawings.

Yours ever,

RUPERT

22 February 1953   *Grundisburgh*

My dear Rupert,

I do hope you will manage somehow to attend the Johnson Club meeting when I have to hold forth. It will be on some day in the last ten days of March. Please let me know if there is any one which you *cannot* manage. I want to be sure of seeing one friendly face in the company. Suppose whenever I look up that I encounter the saurian eye of Dr Chapman? I promise that you shall be next to Roger Fulford[1] who is coming as my guest, whom I *believe* you know, but am quite sure you will like if you don't (an odd sentence).

I hope you flourish. Whenever I see advertised a book I want, it always seems to come from the firm of Hart-Davis. As one might expect.

The winter has been very long in East Anglia—or, as I suspect, there has been more *jaw* about it than usual as about everything. But spring is rubbing its eyes and yawning (yes, I know how Tuppy Headlam[2], did so too—much too often—without at all resembling spring, but you see what I mean).

Gosh, what muck the B.B.C. pours out of an evening. Really those comedians! I am getting sick of Ralph Whiteman—or do I mean Wightman? He talks too much. But I want to send up a question:—Suppose you were on a desert island with Florence Nightingale, Beatrice Webb, Edith Summerskill and a packet

1. The historian.   2. Eton master.

of arsenic, which of the three ladies would be the first to get arsenic, or rather in what order would they *all* get it?

Yours ever,

GEORGE LYTTELTON

P.S. My paper will be thought very flimsy by those old diplodoci, but who cares?

26 *February 1953*   *Grundisburgh*

My dear Rupert,

I am seething! A letter this very morning from the man Marshall the gist of which is that the meeting must be in the first fortnight of *April*, at *luncheon* instead of dinner, and in *Brown's Hotel*—of all places. To feel hovering about us the spirit of Dr Johnson has, if one may say so, something inspiring about it, but what if we exchange it for that of Dr Buchman[1] whose headquarters are in B.H.? That is 'quite another thing', as George III used to reiterate—about almost everything, as far as I remember. Or do you think that the grey and secret soul of Dr Chapman has found its spiritual home in the Oxford Group.

But it is no good cursing. You will, I know, come if you can, and so will Roger F. but I rather fear that at the end of March he will have returned to his fastness in Westmorland.

Yours ever,

GEORGE LYTTELTON

1. Founder of the Oxford Group (Moral Rearmament).

29 *March 1953*   *Grundisburgh*

[POSTCARD]

All is well. Roger Fulford will be there on April 15 and I have asked the man Mitchell to see that he is next to you. For all I know I may be acting *ultra vires*. It may be a rule of more than Athanasian antiquity that one troglodyte is neither greater nor less than another; and that a guest cannot but find his neighbour delightful, whoever he is. But we will manage somehow.

G.W.L.

21 September 1953   *Grundisburgh*

My dear Rupert,

I am delighted to see you are bringing out some letters of old Elwin's[1], which should be very good reading. I have read two volumes of his (since 1906), essays on the XVIIIth century which I have never come across in anyone else's possession. They contain an excellent one on old Johnson. I see the T.L.S. has at last reviewed the Letters. I put up a friend of mine to tell Pryce-Jones that the Johnson Club were rather tight-lipped about the apparent priority given week after week to the work of not very memorable foreigners, and the answer was that the Johnson reviewer refused to be hurried. I thought he did his work very well.[2] The letters increase one's respect and affection for the old man. His courtesy and kindness continuously in evidence, and that majestic honesty and genuineness rising like a great oak above the weeds and suckers—his temper, and table-manners and prejudices and rudeness. And there is plenty of fun too. Surely his lips twitched when he wrote 'Mrs Williams's pimples continue to come and go'? And I love 'Dropsy began to threaten, but seasonable physic stopped the inundation'—which gives his ailment the same stature as the Yangtse or the Ganges as they annually sweep ten thousand oriental families into oblivion.

Meanwhile I hear that our shock-headed secretary is in hospital with some form of polio, poor chap, which, I suppose, is why we didn't meet on the Dr's birthday. I missed you at the June meeting. Dear Dr Chapman had not taken much trouble over his reflections about editing.

I am just back from the village church, where the rector dogmatised freely about mysteries which he did not understand, and the congregation didn't wish to hear. In Suffolk we treat all mysteries as if they were sleeping dogs—not like Dorothy Parker, who, you may remember, says she was sacked from some school for saying that the Immaculate Conception was much the same as Spontaneous Combustion.

1. *A Blessed Girl* (1953). Letters between Lady Emily Lutyens and the Rev. Whitwell Elwin, 1887–96.

2. The reviewer was John Sparrow.

I feel really rather compunctious about writing to you, as you are much too busy to answer gossipy letters. Besides, didn't the great man say 'There is no transaction which offers stronger temptation to sophistication and fallacy than epistolary intercourse.' But I had to write to you. My youngest daughter is to be married here in a few days and the atmosphere is thick with femininity, as the preparations, the clothes, the invitations are endlessly and delightedly discussed. Their chief anxiety is about my i) clothes ii) behaviour at the ceremony. They seem to think I don't know the difference between the vestry and the belfry. The only thing they have no doubt about is my (a) ability and (b) willingness to sign unlimited cheques.

Mind you don't answer this till it is no longer pain and grief.

Yours ever,

GEORGE LYTTELTON

30 November 1953   *Grundisburgh*

My dear Rupert,

Coincidence is very rum. Last Sept. 21 I wrote two letters—one of them to you. Nothing happened till yesterday, when there was a charming letter from you on the breakfast table, and in the day's *Times* the announcement of the other's death, viz Sir Ivor Atkins. Isn't that a bit uncanny? Of course I don't expect you to answer immediately, as I know you will some day; and I saw Roger Fulford who told me that, as I expected, you were busy up to the neck. Very good news. Your Tibet[1] book and *A Blessed Girl* are both on my list. There is no doubt that the Hart-Davis books are the most attractive in the public eye—I mean of course among the more intelligent readers. Are they a growing band or not? You must be trampling on the prone and quivering bodies of your rivals. What I wonder is poor James Barrie going, if not going slowly under? Alas, I cannot manage the Johnson Club on Dec. 11, as I shall be in the middle of exam papers which for some dark reason have to be marked at top

1. *Seven Years in Tibet* by Heinrich Harrer.

151

speed. I wish you had been free on the night I cadged a dinner off Tim Nugent. Then we *should* have had a good crack. You know, Rupert, those old Johnsonians are very insolent. I told you how dull and scrappy that austere veteran R.W.C. was in the summer. He simply hadn't taken *any* trouble. Do you think that the thoughts that flit through the mind while shaving are good enough for us? Given a modicum of intelligence and taste for words anyone can turn out a respectable paper, *if one takes enough trouble.* But these shameless old pedants don't take any.

Last week I attended the centenary dinner of the Ipswich Cricket Club. There were 24 speeches. I made one, as M.C.C. guest, and they took it kindly though it was not in the general pattern, i.e. to say 'Talking of umpires I am reminded of a story I once heard about the parable of the virgins', and then retail an anecdote which might just have passed muster in Fourth Form passage in the reign of good Queen Victoria (not in her hearing of course). The evening lasted from 7.0 till 11.45. Between the toasts a young woman pinned us to the wall with songs of Araby and suchlike. It was all very jolly and boring, as you may imagine, but somehow left an impression of unsophisticated bonhomie which was really very pleasant and English—almost Thomas Hardyish. They were all *fundamentally* more civilised than two Americans at the same table in the restaurant car coming from Italy a month ago, who lit cigars in the middle of their—and our—dinner just to show their superiority to a) good manners and b) the rest of the passengers. They looked like the first and second murderers, though none of the words that squeezed past the cigars sounded at all like 'The west yet glimmers with some streaks of day', as the killer of Banquo put it.

Do you know almost my oldest friend Percy Lubbock, whom I, with another friend, was visiting at his enchanting house at Lerici—the Gulf of Spezia and purple hills and vineyards in one direction, and in the other the Mediterranean, full of craggy islands and shifting sunlight. P.L. is almost quite blind and we did a minute little towards paying our way by a good deal of reading aloud. I forget whether you are as sound as I should wish about P.L.'s *Earlham*, i.e. calmly certain that it is one of the most exquisite books in the English language—and shews the English language to be supreme with Greek on two pinnacles. Or do you think I chuck adjectives about like a peer pro or anti television? The postmaster-general is an old pupil of mine, and is not really quite heavily enough gunned for a full debate. Shall we not have some sad stuff from the advertisers? Not that I have studied the question. My policy—wh. I recommend to you—is to see which side is taken by Lord Brabazon of Tara (ra Boom de Ay) and then take the opposite. The House of Lords has been rather spirited lately. Lord Samuel I suppose had ancestors in Sodom and Gomorrah (but could there be any offspring there?). Old Agate, as no doubt you know, could have warned our panicky legislators years ago. Once, at lunch in the Ivy he glanced round with disillusioned eyes and said, 'My dear chap, there are 15 homosexuals and 5 Lesbians within the flip of a cherrystone.' (I like the blend—very characteristic of J.A., the happy little literary twirl rounding off the heavy coarseness of the dictum—like the necklace of flowers on a shire horse).

Have you followed the affair of the Banned Boy and the Governors of Woodbridge School? I am one of them. It is all political really. The Socialists want all independent schools abolished and no HM to be free to reject candidates. Miss Horsburgh[1] let us down—as we were told she probably would. A small majority increases wariness and diminishes courage.

Do you ever go to America? Not that I want you to, but I *should* like to cable to someone called Ruperto Wesdo. (The 'do' puzzles me; it gives you a sort of Jugo-Slav colouring). When shall we meet again? I have *masses* of things to say to you. This prolix letter only touches the fringe.

Yours ever,

G.W.L.

1. Florence Horsburgh, Conservative Minister of Education.

12 April 1954   *36 Soho Square*

My dear George,

For the first time this year I have wiped off all my arrears of correspondence, and the last item at the bottom of the pile is the enchanting letter that you sent me on November 30th. It went to the bottom because in it you said you didn't expect an early answer, so I hope you will forgive my seeming ingratitude. Last time I belatedly answered one of your letters, it sounded the death knell for another friend of yours and I only hope that such a calamity won't recur.

I see Roger Fulford once a month at the London Library committee and also usually at a Dining Club to which we both belong. I only wish I saw you half as often. I skipped the last Johnson Club meeting, thinking it unlikely that you would be there, and because after your sparkling talk the ditherings of the old professionals seem even more contemptible.

Thank you for all the nice things you say about this firm's books. This last year has been an extremely lucky and prosperous one for us: in which we have not only made our first profit, but have also been able to write off the accumulated losses of the six previous years. With a little more luck we should be on an even keel in two or three years time. I say 'luck' because one book such as *Seven Years in Tibet* can, in only a few months, alter one's whole financial position almost incredibly. We have now sold close on 130,000 copies of that book. Please keep that very much to yourself, since most people think we have sold more!

I saw James Barrie the other day. He seemed cheerful but I can't help feeling that the business must be pretty shaky.

I do indeed know Percy Lubbock, though I think we have only actually met once. I was at Cape's when they published several of his books, and since then we have corresponded a good deal about both Hugh Walpole and Henry James. I was extravagantly proud and delighted when he told me that the whole of my Walpole book had been read aloud to him and had given him pleasure and satisfaction. I would love to go out and read to him myself but, alas, I have neither time nor money. P.L. and one of my aunts (now dead) were childhood playmates—if not sweethearts—and I possess a manuscript book containing composite poems of theirs. I have always held *Earlham* to be a masterpiece, and a future classic.

I am sorry you are upset by my 'Wesdo'. There are endlessly

complicated rules about cable addresses one may adopt; it has to be so many letters etc. etc. After a great deal of correspondence with the Post Office they agreed on 'Ruperto' but insisted on adding the code-word 'Wesdo' to say which part of London we are in. I do go to America, but the visits consume so much time and energy that I try and let someone else go if possible. It looks now as if I may have to go in the autumn of 1955.

My best news at the moment is that my elder boy has just been elected to Pop. He has two more Halves to go and is, as you can imagine, tremendously excited. He has only got his House Colours and his Sixpenny, but was unlucky to miss both his Lower Club and his Rugger Fifteen by one place. I'm afraid he won't be good enough for the Eleven next Half, but I have a sneaking hope that he may get his XXII—rather an anticlimax of a Colour, I always feel, except for playing at Upper Club on the Fourth of June. He has already an O.S., and will be in sixth form his last Half, so altogether I think he can be said to have done well, and I get tremendous vicarious satisfaction out of his success, having myself been totally undistinguished at Eton, wearing a scug cap all my days.

We simply must meet soon. When are you next coming to London? You may not recognise me when we meet since I have recently been through a rigorous course of dieting, lost well over a stone and for a change now look more like Slender than Falstaff.

Yours ever,
RUPERT

18 April 1954   *Grundisburgh*

My dear Rupert,

How nice of you to write—from the heart of the typhoon, so to speak, where for a short deceptive moment there is peace. It is *very* good news to hear that the firm is really prosperous, though if you weren't, who, a' God's name, would be? It must be a very bewildering job—so impossible to guess what the great ass, the public, is going to take to its vague and shapeless bosom.

I greatly enjoyed *Seven Y in T* but should not have had any notion on first seeing it that it would be a best seller. In fact my judgement is just about on a level with that of the majority of critics of today—though to be sure, a good critic, according to Housman, is at least as rare as a good poet. Do you remember that delightfully characteristic sentence in his Stephen Lecture: 'In the last thirty years I have improved in some respects and deteriorated in others, but I have not improved so much as to become a good critic, or deteriorated so much as to think I am one.' And with that I hope both F. R. and Queenie Leavis slunk home with their long ears replete with fleas.

I always feel sorry for James Barrie in what must be a very uphill journey. Didn't he lose L. P. Hartley's last book because L.P.H. found his previous ones were insufficiently advertised? If you can't afford to advertise, you sell little, and if you sell little you can't afford etc. The perfect example of the vicious circle— as good as an old favourite of mine—slightly disgusting—of the man who sweated into his soup because it was so hot; and the more soup he drank, the more . . . but you see how the repulsive circle closes. Anyway I shall certainly send to you, and not J.B, my blank verse epic on medieval Suffolk. After all it was your charitable and infectious laughter at my paper last year that wreathed old Chapman's face in smiles—the modern equivalent of 'creating a soul under the ribs of death.' I too shirked that Johnson lunch, feeling sure that you were not going to be there. I wonder if they have made any new members. With medical science making such strides there must be plenty of nonagenarians about. I once proposed Christopher Hollis, but R.W.C. would have none of him. Couldn't we have another try? I remember him as a very able and friendly fellow; and he wrote a book on Johnson that was very readable. But I grant you he has barely if at all reached the green and callow fifties.

Mind you call on P. Lubbock if you are ever in Italy. He would immensely like it. Any O.E. is always welcome—not perhaps the Lord Rosebery or Buns Cartwright, or even the late Lionel Tennyson, but the reasonably civilised. And if you insist on talking Italian and giving the name Ruperto Wesdo, you'll be equally welcome.

I have two sons-in-law here, both Eton masters, and they both speak very well of your elder boy. He sounds just the right sort of chap. I think I met him briefly at Fred Coleridge's Boys' Dinner, but *all* his high table seemed to be sons of old pupils of mine so that I was rather in a whirl. *I* was once President of Pop, and I remember insisting on the ballot for new members being secret, which it hadn't been for years. This I did not wholly from highmindedness and public spirit, but chiefly to get Alec Cadogan in—I forget quite how it worked. He was the first scug cap ever to get in—so it was clear I was a great reformer, though I cannot remember anyone recognising the fact at the time.

I will get in touch with you in the early summer, and look out for a slim, not to say svelte figure. I go about with a stick nowadays, having a hip-joint which my specialist bluntly says is incurable. It doesn't bother me, and a good deal of his bluntness, I think, is because of my telling him that his butler had made the appointment on the 'phone, and it was really his wife. I just did not say: 'Well anyway, she has the voice of Paul Robeson.' Such are the pitfalls of life.

Yours ever,

GEORGE LYTTELTON

5 October 1954   *36 Soho Square*

My dear George,

A thousand thanks for your delicious letter of October 1st. [missing]. It has made me laugh out loud on a Monday morning! I am indeed going to the Johnson Club dinner on Friday, and look forward to seeing you there. De Beer is going to address us on Indexing—he has spent goodness knows how many years indexing his new edition of Evelyn's Diary—and I am bringing two guests: Humphry House (of Wadham) who is editing Dickens's complete correspondence for me, and Jim Thornton (of the B.B.C.) who is going to index it. For heaven's sake let us all cling together.

Yours ever, RUPERT

9 October 1955   *Grundisburgh*

My dear Rupert,

This is just a line to say I *hope* you will be among the Johnsonians on Thursday and doing what you always do to blunt the effect on the atmosphere and company of dear Drs Chapman and Powell—and one or two other ancients whose names I have never yet discovered. I don't know who is addressing us, but I know one very definite thing about it viz that it will be more interesting than de Beer on indexing. Though I see they knighted him for it—unless *Sir Gavin* is somebody else[1]. The christian name is surely very incongruous, calling up as it does a medieval world of joust and tourney. What would Sir Lancelot have made of indexing?

I am delighted to see that you have L. E. Jones's *Stings and Honey* (which I have immediately ordered). I hope that means he has left Secker and Warburg who I thought ought to have republished some of the early L.E.J.'s when everyone was talking of his *Victorian Boyhood*. But a reading public which lets a book of such quality as *A la Carte* go out of print is I suppose to be expected in these days. Do you remember the pastiche, the deathbed of Edward VII as Lytton Strachey would have described it, when they just caught, or seemed to catch, his last words: 'Don't let poor Cassel starve.' That alone makes the little book immortal, apart from the superb shot at what Johnson would have said on hearing that a solicitor had been made H.M. of Rugby—'Why, Sir, an attorney may be a very good sort of man, but you are not to govern boys with writs of Mandamus.' Surely that would get a smile of appreciation from our two Drs?

I hope you and the great firm are both flourishing, if that is not a big word to use in 1955. I am rapidly reaching that dreary but almost inevitable reach of senility which Tuppy Headlam had got to when much younger, viz the firm belief, or conviction, that *every* change, great or small, is for the worse. How shocked my hostess was when her insistence on my adding some saying to my signature in her blasted Visitors Book stung me

1. It was another Gavin de Beer (zoologist and historian).

into writing that from Jeremiah—'The heart is deceitful above all things, and desperately wicked.' She thought it was dreadfully pessimistic. But was it?

Yours ever,

GEORGE LYTTELTON

———————

NOTES

CHARLES DENNIS FISHER (1877-1916) was the sixth son of Herbert William Fisher, vice-warden of the Stannaries. His elder brothers included H. A. L. Fisher, the historian, and Admiral Sir William Fisher who was unamused by his cousin Virginia Woolf's participation in the 'Dreadnought Hoax'. His sister Adeline married the composer Ralph Vaughan Williams. The Fishers lived at Blatchington Court, Seaford, Sussex.

From Westminster School Charles Fisher went to Christ Church as a scholar. He played cricket for Oxford and Sussex in 1900. He became Censor (lay equivalent of Dean) of Christ Church and edited Tacitus for the Clarendon Press.

At the outbreak of war, disabled from joining a fighting regiment, he went to Flanders with the R.A.M.C. (motor ambulances) and was mentioned in dispatches. Then, after a brief training, he joined *H.M.S. Invincible*, 'the mother of warships', as lieutenant.

When, at the Battle of Jutland, she was blown up with the loss of 1026 lives, the only survivor, Commander Dannreuther, reported that Fisher was by his side during the battle and 'in the highest spirits, having under his control some part of the mechanism for the direction of firing.' He was 38.

The poet laureate Robert Bridges dedicated a poem, 'The Chivalry of the Sea' to his memory.

GWL's essay was privately printed by Stanley Morison at the Pelican Press.

In Memoriam G. W. H. by A. B. R. [†]

Autumn shows varied splendours, and with gold
The woods sign that the year is passing by.
We too are worn by the long age allowed us;
We too well know that death must have its due.
As leaves are fallen so companions fall
To silence and surcease, O Tuppy wise.
Now that your voice is hushed, we too are silent,
Longing for you who pleased us as a friend.
You laughed or grieved: your many comrades now
Celebrate you with laughter as with tears.
These friends are here; these well-loved haunts around;
Painter and poet, you are with us still.
Remembering how you filled all things with joy,
With witty talk, with honest countenance,
We lay you here in old delights, and Eton
Guards on her breast, mother for loyal son,
One dear to all, whom Truth and Goodness own
As one who truly loved them while he lived.
Your country too proclaims your gallantry,
And as you go great trumpets sound their welcome.

B. W. M. Y.

[†] See rear endpaper.
G. W. Headlam (nicknamed Tuppy) and A. B. Ramsay
were both Eton masters.

ACKNOWLEDGEMENTS

For help with this book, grateful thanks are due to Lady Hart-Davis, Mrs Peter Lawrence, Viscount Cobham, and Sir Paul Getty, K.B.E. Sir Brian Young provided a blank verse translation of the Latin poem on the rear endpaper. For permission to reprint part of John Betjeman's poem 'Christmas' acknowledgement is made to John Murray Ltd.; and to the estate of Frances Cornford for 'In the Backs' and 'For A.S. sleeping when Old'. Duff Hart-Davis and Humphrey Lyttelton kindly gave permission for the early Lyttelton Hart-Davis letters to be published. George Ramsden, 'onlie begetter' of this project, also did most of the editing. Any mistakes are his.